Influence with Respect

INFLUENCE
with RESPECT

Carsten Hjorth Pedersen

Translated by Peter Weber Vindum
Illustrated by Helle Høeg

RESOURCE *Publications* • Eugene, Oregon

INFLUENCE WITH RESPECT

Copyright © 2020 Carsten Hjorth Pedersen. All rights reserved. Except for brief quotations in critical publications or reviews, no part of this book may be reproduced in any manner without prior written permission from the publisher. Write: Permissions, Wipf and Stock Publishers, 199 W. 8th Ave., Suite 3, Eugene, OR 97401.

Resource Publications
An Imprint of Wipf and Stock Publishers
199 W. 8th Ave., Suite 3
Eugene, OR 97401

www.wipfandstock.com

PAPERBACK ISBN: 978-1-7252-5660-6
HARDCOVER ISBN: 978-1-7252-5661-3
EBOOK ISBN: 978-1-7252-5662-0

Manufactured in the U.S.A.   JUNE 25, 2020

Originally published by Credo and LogosMedia Publishers, Korskærvej 25, 7000 Fredericia, Denmark under the title: *Påvirk med respekt*

Bible text is cited from The Holy Bible, English Standard Version® (ESV®) Copyright © 2001 by Crossway, a publishing ministry of Good News Publishers. All rights reserved.

CONTENTS

Preface | vii

Chapter 1
THE COMPLEX WORLD OF INFLUENCE | 1

Chapter 2
A THEORETICAL AND PRACTICAL MODEL | 14

Chapter 3
FURTHER PERSPECTIVES ON INTIMIZATION, DESERTION, CONFRONTATION, AND WITHDRAWAL | 32

Chapter 4
THE IMPORTANCE OF CONFRONTATION | 44

Chapter 5
RELIGIOUS EXTREMISM | 56

Chapter 6
WHAT OPTIONS DO PARENTS, TEACHERS, AND PREACHERS HAVE? | 76

Chapter 7
WHAT CAN CHILDREN, STUDENTS, AND LISTENERS DO? | 86

Chapter 8
LOVE REQUIRES NEARNESS AND DISTANCE | 97

Bibliography | 101
About the Author | 103

PREFACE

BEING ABLE TO PUBLISH this book in English is a great joy to me, as it makes it accessible to a broader audience compared to its two Danish predecessors from 2007 and 2019. It is my sincere wish that my model for how to influence with respect will be a helpful tool for those who influence others, and for those who are subject to such influence.

The book is rooted in a range of interviews with adults who, as children or young adults, experienced both positive and negative forms of influence. In considering these experiences, I draw on educational and psychological theory as well as examples from film, literature, and our daily human interaction. And last but not least, I look to my own years of experience as a parent, teacher, mentor, and preacher.

AUDIENCE

The book is aimed at everyone who influences children, young people, and adults (i.e., parents, teachers, educators, preachers, club leaders, etc.).

Although the book's primary audience is Christians, it is my view the challenge is at least as great for Muslims, atheists, agnostics, and relativists. In fact, it is my impression that especially agnostics and relativists face a great challenge when it comes to influencing with respect, and I hope those who place themselves

PREFACE

in one of these categories will be open to the ideas presented in this book.

Also, the book is aimed at those who are being—or have been—influenced, with or without respect. It is my hope that this group will find clarification in relation to the impact of this influence, as well as a language they can use to talk about it. I am thinking in particular of those who have experienced letdowns in the sphere of influence. I hope this book can help them overcome the challenge of moving on. Finally, it is my prayer that those who predominantly have been influenced with respect will see how privileged they are and contemplate how to pass that privilege on to others.

BUT WHY DO WE NOT JUST AVOID INFLUENCE?

Although we are only in the preface, this is a relevant question to ask. Is the problem not the impact itself? Is the root of the problem not the very fact that we *want* to influence other people in the first place?

In short, I do not think so, and I will give a more detailed justification for this viewpoint in the following pages. But in general there are four reasons why noninfluence does not solve the problem:

1) Noninfluence does not exist. Human life is so interrelated that neutrality is an impossibility. Influence is a fundamental premise in human life. Everyone affects their children. Everyone affects the people they speak to. Even relativists influence their surroundings. We simply cannot help it. Rather, the question is whether or not we do it with respect.

2) Children and teenagers can only experience healthy and independent development by encountering the adult generation's best take on the good life. We simply have to influence our children if we want them to become independent adults. We have to give them something they can either accept or reject.

Although this seems paradoxical, it is a reality everyone with an educational responsibility must come to terms with.

3) Even those who advocate a religiously neutral education, or claim children must choose their faith without any outside influence, influence others. They do not lead them toward a particular belief system, but toward the mainstream culture's agnosticism and relativism. The only difference is the minority's indoctrination, social control, and coercion are easier to spot than the majority's. Therefore, influencing with respect is very important for both minorities and majorities.

4) In recent years, great emphasis has been placed on religious extremism and social control, i.e., the fact that certain—often religious—environments exert great social pressure to keep children and young people from altering their worldview. In several cases, individuals are even excluded from their community due to a change of conviction. But mostly we see a milder version, where children are merely isolated from various sources of influence. The term "religious extremism" is primarily used in relation to Muslim communities, but Christian communities are increasingly experiencing similar accusations. To face this problem we have to learn how to influence with respect.

It is my intention that this book will help clarify a critical issue, but above all, I hope it will be a helping hand to all the parents, teachers, educators, club leaders, preachers, and others who read it. It is my hope even more children, teenagers, young adults, and grown-ups will become part of the constructive reciprocity that characterizes respectful influence.

Carsten Hjorth Pedersen
Hillerød, Denmark, March, 2020

CHAPTER 1

THE COMPLEX WORLD OF INFLUENCE

THIS BOOK WRESTLES WITH an issue I am sure is familiar to every parent, teacher, and preacher across cultures, as well as to all children, teenagers, and students. As human beings, our basic intuition tells us there are both positive and negative forms of influence. However, it is those who primarily carry with them the negative experiences who are able to most accurately describe the difference between the two forms.

This became evident to me during my preparations for the interview survey I repeatedly return to in this book. I conducted a range of preliminary interviews, but I only spoke to young adults who had no significant experience with negative influencing during their school years. It was difficult for them to acknowledge their own privileged position, which made it hard for them to articulate the exact difference between positive and negative influence.

However, as I got to speak to informants who had experienced both sides, I got a much more nuanced description of the distinctive features that separate "influence in the positive way" from "influence in the negative way." These informants provided me with the terminology I use in the models presented in this book.

So let me open this chapter with the words of two of my informants, whose names and circumstances will remain anonymous.

Afterward, I will give the floor to two other individuals who carry equally valuable experiences.

FOUR INDIVIDUAL EXPERIENCES

Peter, who attended a Christian free school:

> There was a correct answer to every question, and that was it. The adults would explain how everything ought to be understood. No nuance or uncertainty was ever allowed into the discussion. We were taught that terrible things would happen to those who left our community. My aunt was a member of the Pentecostal Church, and she was considered a lost soul. . . . In this context, faith is something that is forced on you. It is stuffed down your throat to such an extent that it no longer has anything to do with personal faith—it is just something you've been taught—something others have told you. There is no personal aspect. . . . The gospel was not in focus, only the rules. We were never allowed to be joyful Christians. The word of God was something that should be shared without joy.[1]

Bridget, who went to a Christian boarding school:

> I reacted to the fact that they [the teachers] were so enclosed in their thinking. Very finalized and very settled. Also, I was triggered by the experience of them becoming much bigger than me in a sense. It became a form of power. When I see a teacher teaching, I see an act of power rather than an act of care and concern.[2]

A fourteen-year-old girl's voice message on the Children's Telephone Helpline[3]:

> My parents are hardcore members of Jehovah's Witnesses, and I experience it as harmful. . . . I want to leave my

 1. Pedersen, *Påvirkning med respekt*, 80.
 2. Pedersen, *Påvirkning med respekt*, 81.
 3. The Children's Telephone Helpline is an anonymous helpline for Danish children.

faith, but I know that if I do so, a large part of my family, if not all of them, will push me away. I fear the outcome, and I would like to speak to someone outside Jehovah's Witnesses and get their perspective.[4]

An eleven-year-old girl's voice message on the Children's Telephone Helpline:

> I am a Muslim, and I am not allowed to do anything. I mean this in a literal sense. I am only allowed to go to school, come back home, help my mother clean the house, and pray to our god. Apart from that, I'm just bored. When I ask if I can go out and play, the answer is always no.[5]

To some extent, the psychology of influence is the same when dealing with children, teenagers, and adults. Naturally, the responsibility is greater in relation to small children, and as you get older your personal responsibility grows in terms of what forms of influence you allow.

A MATTER OF FORM

There is an important difference between "negative influence" and "being influenced in a negative manner." The former is primarily a matter of content, while the latter is a matter of form or method.

Most people would probably agree if you teach your children to lie or steal—perhaps because you do it yourself—it is an example of negative influence. But whether or not it is a negative influence to teach your children there is a God or the Republicans have the most reasonable policy cannot be determined objectively. It is a matter of conviction, faith, and assessment.

Influence in a negative manner often occurs in questions pertaining to conviction, faith, and assessment. For instance, it is usually less relevant to talk about influence in a positive or negative manner in areas such as math or geography.

4. *Adfærdskontrol og tankefængsel*, 49.
5. *Adfærdskontrol og tankefængsel*, 29.

Since we all have certain convictions—even if we are not aware of them—it is not the conviction itself that is problematic. It can be false or untrue, but that is a different issue. But the *manner* in which we are convinced and pass on that conviction can be more or less positive, appropriate, or legitimate. In short, it is a matter of *form*.

However, form and content are not two completely detached elements. If your conviction tends to be sharp and narrow, it becomes all the more important to be aware of influencing with respect. Therefore, this is especially a challenge among the minority. It might seem unfair, but minority communities simply have to accept this fact and take it into account when navigating within the sphere of influence.

The majority, however, finds itself in a different and perhaps even more serious danger—namely the danger of not being aware of its own biased values. Often the majority is blind to the fact there is no evidence to support their value systems, and they unconsciously pass those values on to younger generations. This is also true for even the most relativistic and agnostic majority groups.

IT GOES BOTH WAYS

Whether it is through teaching, supervision, or preaching, adults constantly influence the children around them, and adults also influence other adults through the same means—but the influencing always goes both ways.

Children also influence the adults around them through their personality and their independent contributions and reactions. Adults who are being influenced by other adults have the possibility of, as well as the responsibility to, test and challenge that influence. Influencing others is not like pouring water into a bottle. If I treat the other person as a mere object for my own influence, then I have overstepped a red line in the sphere of influence. There *is* and *ought to be* reciprocity whenever we move within the sphere of influence.

Therefore, the following pages will explore the issue of *reciprocity* in relation to influence. Although the main focus is on the role of the influencer, we will also find time to reflect on how we teach ourselves and our children to handle the influence we get exposed to.

INFLUENCE THROUGH THE MEDIA

In our everyday lives, we are not only influenced through direct encounters with other people, such as the encounter between children and parents at home, or between an audience and a preacher.

To an increasing extent, influencing takes place in arenas that on the surface appear more neutral, such as TV and social media. On some level, we are aware there are real people behind the output—someone produced the newspaper I am reading, someone created the cartoon my child is watching. There is a real individual behind the post on Instagram or Facebook. But most of the time this other, or these others, are more or less anonymous. So how should we approach this more indirect form of influence, and can we even talk about influencing with or without respect through various forms of audiovisual media?

I believe we can, but we do have to take a different approach. Both positive and negative influence are very much about the direct, face-to-face encounter between two individuals. Fundamentally, influencing is a matter of interaction, and as we will discover later on, empathy and maturity are key elements in this process.

Therefore, the legitimacy of media-based influencing lies on a different level. Naturally, the nature of the content is still a factor—Are we dealing with a positive message with a legitimate purpose?—but to truly evaluate whether or not the media influences with respect we have to consider the *methods* they apply.

When watching TV, movies, and online streaming services, we must ask ourselves if the issues and themes they treat are presented fairly and without bias. Does a movie contain hidden commercials and product placement? Do the producers have a hidden agenda that unconsciously affects us? Perhaps the influence is strongest when we drop our guards and merely allow ourselves to be entertained.

When it comes to social media, the crucial challenge is to question the legitimacy of online identities. Are the various social fora just echo chambers that merely confirm our beliefs and prejudices? Do platforms like Instagram promote an unhealthy and self-centered culture? And what should we think about the Facebook algorithms designed to generate profit through marketing and sales?

The criteria underlying the influence of the media are different from those underlying face-to-face encounters. This book focuses on the latter, but there is no doubt the influence of the media is of vital importance today. Therefore, I urge those who have the necessary skills and knowledge to take up the challenge of analyzing to what extent the influencing of the media is conducted *with* or *without* respect.

MINORITY OR MAJORITY

Often, when the majority within a community shares an opinion, that opinion tends to be seen as a self-evident fact, while the opinions of the minority are merely seen as subjective convictions. Let us take *hedonism* as an example.

Hedonism is the idea that *pleasure is the fundamental purpose of life*. This idea is highly prevalent today. In our daily lives, we focus a lot on increasing our own well-being. Life is about enjoyment and prosperity. Therefore, entertainment, freedom from pain, and material wealth are fundamental values in our lives. This approach to life has become so self-evident we see it as a matter of course—until, for instance, we read about ancient Sparta and the Spartans who were known for their toughness, their austere lifestyle, and their willingness to be self-sacrificial. When encountering such an alternative approach to life, we realize hedonism is not a self-evident choice, but an ideological position that has gained ground in modern society due to historical, psychological, and sociological circumstances.

Discussing the legitimacy of various forms of influence is irrelevant in monocultures or highly isolated cultures, which for instance have no access to mass media. Such cultures live in (blissful?) ignorance of the challenges and dangers of influence. However, the question of positive and negative influence becomes highly relevant in pluralistic societies, where facts, interpretations, and ideologies are constantly changing, and where it is difficult to distinguish one idea or worldview from another. In these societies, the spotlight often falls on those who diverge most significantly from the opinions of the majority.

THE WILL TO INFLUENCE

It is a precondition for this book that influencing is a real phenomenon—not just according to a simple model where a sender transmits a message to a receiver but as a far more complex mechanism.

The message or content is not a clearly defined element either. Although often unintended, a message always carries with it a range of underlying messages, and the sender must always be aware that the receiver's perception of the content differs from the sender's own perception. Every communicative situation contains a range of elements that cannot be controlled.

Today, we often see parents, teachers, and preachers who have *no desire* to influence. But a central claim in this book is this can never be avoided, and the first step is to accept that we influence each other constantly—even through the things we choose *not* to say or do. Therefore, the message of this book is we must be *willing* to influence, but *with respect*.

I wish to challenge the idea that we help our children, our young adults, and our listeners by not wanting to affect their lives. My point is this tendency unwillingly makes us bearers of a growing relativism which is already far too dominating throughout Western culture. But I also argue we do others a favor by wanting something specific for them—because the explicit message is always easier to relate to than the vague or implicit message. To put it simply, it is always better to encounter people who care.

Either we consciously influence others with a specific intention, or we influence them unconsciously, without knowing what we communicate and without providing the receiver with a foundation for assessing that influence. The German education theorist Klaus Mollenhauer puts it like this:

> To the extent that we live together with children, we also share our lives with them—anything else is impossible. We cannot erase ourselves as social beings; we cannot assume a dead or neutral position. This truth is indeed trivial, but nonetheless it is the primary and most serious reality within the field of education. Upbringing is primarily a matter of transmission; communication of our own fundamental values. There can be no act of education in which the adult does not communicate something about himself and his own way of life, whether it is intentional or unintentional.[6]

INFLUENCE THROUGH UPBRINGING AND EDUCATION

In this book, I choose to focus on the nature of influence within three specific arenas: Upbringing, education, and preaching. Keeping these three concepts separate is no easy task as they all overlap and intertwine with each other. Despite the difficulties in drawing a clear line between them, we can still describe their qualities separately and therefore the distinction will turn out to be both meaningful and helpful.

For lack of a better alternative, I use the word "upbringing" to translate the more complex Danish word *opdragelse*, which merges the meaning of "upbringing" and "education," and is similar to the German *Erziehung*. The intention of *opdragelse* or *Erziehung* is twofold, namely, to teach the child certain skills and influence his or her opinions.

Reidar Myhre, one of Norway's most important education theorists of the late twentieth century, has given us the following

---

6. Mollenhauer, *Glemte sammenhenger*, 22.

definition of *opdragelse*, i.e., upbringing, which will also be helpful in this context:

> By the term *upbringing* we refer to the individual adult's, as well as the entire adult generation's, attempt to transmit to the younger generations—under mutual influence—the knowledge and skills, opinions and attitudes, and social and religious practices that define the social and cultural context in which the upbringing takes place—and to do this in such a manner that the new generation is assisted in using their abilities and possibilities in the areas of human compassion, responsibility and independence, so that they can give back to society and culture in a manner that is both stabilizing and creative.[7]

With this very broad definition, upbringing also comes to contain the general socialization of children and young adults that takes place at home as well as in various institutions and church communities.

Although Myhre sees education as something that lies within the broader concept of upbringing, he maintains education is a unique form of upbringing. Myhre gives the following definition of education:

> The decisive trait when defining *education* is that education seeks to develop the intellect and skills of young people by means of planned and systematic guidance from adults through acquisition of knowledge, empathy, practice, and the student's own effort. . . . In general, we can say that the difference between upbringing and education becomes increasingly evident the more the education is systematized and intellectualized. In turn, it becomes increasingly difficult to distinguish the upbringing from the education the more the education is integrated into the practices of everyday life.[8]

---

7. Myhre, *Hva er pedagogikk?*, 45 (emphasis mine).
8. Myhre, *Innføring i pedagogikk 2*, 41–42 (emphasis his).

Apart from upbringing and education, I find it reasonable to include a third concept in our consideration of the nature of influence, namely preaching. This claim calls for further explanation.

INFLUENCE THROUGH PREACHING

Let me begin by making it clear that preaching, ideally, is unrelated to the exercise of pressure or force:

> Like proper education, proper preaching represents the direct opposite of pressure and propaganda. Preaching is directed at the human being as an individual. It is directed at the individual person, and it seeks to call him or her into personal freedom and responsibility. Preaching seeks to liberate the individual from all ties, whether conventional, political or ideological. It leads us into responsibility as it confronts us with Jesus' challenging question: "Who do you say I am?" In this sense, teaching and interpretation are matters of "speaking *about*" and "speaking *with*," through which demands and personal appeals can be said to come into play indirectly; preaching, on the other hand, is a matter of "speaking *to*" and contains an unavoidable: And I tell you![9]

Today, preaching is not only found in religious contexts. It has become a common form of communication, which in some contexts is used as a synonym for engagement and personal commitment. Although this is a part of what preaching means, there is much more to it than just engagement.

If we want to move closer to a pedagogical use of the word preaching, it is more productive to consider the mode of influence in which a speaker explicitly addresses people in the form of monologue.

We know this form of communication from political speeches. The setting might be a political convention or a political debate. We find the same form of communication in motivational

---

9. Hvas, *Folkeskolens kristendomsundervisning*, 151–52 (emphasis original).

speeches, such as when a leader of a demonstration seeks to create a uniform, collective response from the crowd. We also see it in the courtroom where the individual who is on trial is referred to as "the accused," and where the sentence is "declared." In all these examples, we are dealing with an explicit, personal, monologue appeal.

This form of influence, based on a direct, personal appeal, comes with a significant responsibility, especially when dealing with children. This, however, does not mean it should be renounced, as it also contains a long range of unique, positive qualities. Rather, it means we must handle it carefully in order to ensure our children learn to navigate safely within it.

The influencing of children is always both implicit and explicit. It is fundamentally implicit, but the explicit element is unavoidable. It is evident that the silent influence of our daily actions and attitudes, although it has a strong effect, must also be accompanied by a verbal and explicit influence. I refer to the most verbal and explicit form of influence as preaching.

But the concept of preaching is not merely defined by its *form*. In an educational context, we also define preaching by its *content*, which is often characterized by a communication of convictions, beliefs, and matters relating to our moral conscience. We often encounter these issues in the areas of religion, politics, and ethics.

PREACHING VERSUS TEACHING

The relationship between preaching and teaching can be clarified in the following manner:

1. Preaching is primarily conducted through monologue, while teaching is essentially dialogic. In other words, the "speaking *to*" is more significant within preaching, while the "speaking *about*" and "speaking *with*" are the primary features of teaching. However, it is important to point out preaching should also contain an element of dialogue and conversation, and

teaching also should be open to elements of monologue and direct, personal appeal.

2. Another determining factor is the communicator's own position in relation to the subject matter. When preaching, the speaker personally vouches for the content, while the teacher maintains a personal distance between himself and the subject matter. Thus, the sphere of preaching is predominantly personal, while the teacher seeks a more objective approach. That being said, only a poor preacher does not keep some degree of distance between himself and the subject matter, and, in turn, every teacher needs a degree of personal engagement in order to teach well.

3. Teaching and preaching also differ in terms of the possible reactions from the receivers. In the context of preaching, the receivers are primarily listeners, but theses listeners must be presented with a free choice between accepting and rejecting the message. In the context of teaching, however, it is not acceptance and rejection but critical response that must be regarded as the primary reaction. Again, we are not dealing with an either/or scenario.

4. Finally, the criteria for determining the truth-value of the subject matter differ within the spheres of preaching and teaching. When teaching, we primarily apply a scientific or humanistic/hermeneutic approach to the concept of truth, while in preaching we turn to an existentialist understanding of truth. In more simple terms, we might say teaching functions on the level of evidence, while preaching functions on the level of conviction. But even here, a certain overlap is unavoidable. Our evidence depends on our convictions, and our convictions are affected by the evidence. Both conceptions of truth must therefore be carefully considered and debated.

We can compress these considerations into the following model that illustrates the fluid boundaries between the two concepts:

	teaching	<------>	preaching
Content—**type**	fact/interpretation	<------>	ideology
Content—**concept of truth**	scientific	<------>	existential
Form—**type**	"speaking *with*" and "speaking *about*"	<------>	"speaking *to*"
Form—**role of communicator**	factual approach	<------>	personal approach
Form—**receiver reaction**	critical response	<------>	rejection/ acceptance

Taking the first line as an example, this is how we should read the model: when considering the type of content, teaching is *primarily* based on facts and interpretation, while preaching *primarily* is based on ideology. However, teaching is never free from ideology, as preaching is never fully detached from facts and interpretations. On this basis, I suggest the following definition:

> **Preaching**: A form of influence mainly concerned with faith, conviction, and ethics, and primarily delivered in the form of explicit, personal address, accompanied by a high degree of freedom to either accept or reject the message.

The four individuals who began this chapter have experienced influence in its negative form, either in the context of upbringing, teaching, or preaching. But what exactly went wrong in these specific cases, and what can we do to replace these mistakes with respectful influence? These are the questions that the following pages seek to address.

Chapter 2

A THEORETICAL AND PRACTICAL MODEL

My original model, first presented in my book *Impact with Respect* from 2007, aimed to describe the distinct relationship between students and their teachers. Since then, I have come to realize the model is equally relevant in other contexts in which we influence each other—such as our homes, day care facilities, and churches.

Therefore, the model presented here takes a broader perspective by simply referring to its two actors as A and B, where A is the person who influences, while B is the one being influenced. In most cases, A is an adult, while B can be a child, a teenager, a young adult, or a grown-up, either in the role of fellow man, student, or listener.

Throughout this book, I speak of A as carrying a *pedagogical responsibility* for B. For instance, parents carry a pedagogical responsibility for their children, as do teachers for their students, kindergarten teachers for their toddlers, preachers for their listeners, and youth group leaders for their teenagers.

There is always an element of pedagogical power at play in the encounter between A and B but in this context the word "power" does not carry any patronizing connotations. In fact, a pedagogical relationship is always a power relationship. The central question is: *To what extent* is power a factor in the relationship, and how do we utilize that power? Do we use it in a legitimate or illegitimate manner?

Impact with Respect presented interviews with seven adults about their school years. The main focus was the religious and political influence the informants experienced as students at either Christian or socialist private independent schools. Alongside various scientific studies, films, and novels, these interviews helped me formulate some of the potential dangers when navigating the space of pedagogical influence. In short, I concluded things go wrong when the person who carries the pedagogical responsibility either comes too close or remains too distant. I refer to the former tendency as *intimization* and the latter as *desertion*. Let me begin this chapter by introducing these two concepts in greater detail.

INTIMIZATION

Intimization is related to intimidation, but the two concepts are not identical.

Intimidation means to instill fear or to scare. Intimization, on the other hand, comes from the word intimate, which means familiar, personal, heartfelt and intrusive. Thus, intimization means becoming too intimate with the person for whom you carry a pedagogical responsibility. It means stepping too close to the child, student, or listener, or entering into someone's most private sphere without having been invited in. This form of intrusion is serious in relation to adults, but it is particularly serious in relation to children, who, due to their immaturity and dependence on adults, are not able to protect themselves in such situations.

In this book, I define intimization thusly:

> **Intimization**: When an individual who carries a pedagogical responsibility, through words or actions, brings his or her influences too close to another person.

Intimization can be illustrated like this:

Fig. 1

We all recognize this "coming too close" as a strong feeling of discomfort when a person comes too near to us *physically*. There is a clear physical limit to how close we want others to come to us, and *mentally* we have a similar limitation. This also applies to children, but their challenge is they are not yet able to sufficiently define and protect these personal boundaries.

Our limit of intimacy is difficult to define. It varies from person to person, from place to place, from environment to environment, from family to family, and from one era of history to another. Not even on an individual level is this limit static. This explains why the line surrounding B in figure 1 is sinuous.

Before we move on, I should mention intimization, in this context, does not apply to criminal matters such as incest or violence, but only to matters regarding the daily interaction between A and B. These are matters that are relevant to all A individuals, whether they are parents, teachers, or church leaders working with children.

Whether or not we choose to use words such as *abuse* or *violation* as synonyms for intimization is a matter of personal language usage. In any case, intimization is defined as a verbal or mental transgression of B's personal limits. From B's perspective, we might describe it as being verbally, mentally, or spiritually bulldozed.

But is it possible for B to *feel* intimized without it being the case?

If we define intimization as a fully subjective term, then it is B alone who decides whether or not an intimization has taken place: If a person *feels* intimized then that person has been intimized.

Naturally, a therapist must base his or her approach entirely on the experience and emotions of the individual. In this book, however, the primary focus is on upbringing, education, and communication, not therapy. My aim is to describe a phenomenon through a general approach in order to create a foundation for public debate. Therefore, I seek to present the central concepts as objectively as possible.

Of course, the subjective experience is extremely important and must never be underestimated, but in order to describe and define a concept the external observer must also have a say. The subjective approach is limited to the subject itself, while the objective aspects can be gathered and examined to form the basis for a discussion and evaluation by several subjects. If we cannot make such objective observations, then we only have the singular experiences left, which we can then take a personal stand on—but the foundation for rational discussion will remain absent.

Therefore, I allow myself to make a clear distinction between *feeling* intimized and *being* intimized. In making this distinction, I see the individual experience as paramount, although I also allow myself to make a mildly objectifying assessment. In the following pages, I will describe the necessary criteria for making such assessments.

DESERTION

One of the most interesting findings in the aforementioned interviews is the informants had not only felt betrayed if their teachers came too close but also if their teachers moved too far away from them and sought to *avoid* influence. I call this phenomenon *desertion*.

While intimization is about A getting too close to B, desertion is about A moving too far away from B. Traditionally, a deserter is a soldier who abandons his post or duty and refuses to fill his position in the army. The word "desertion" comes from the Latin word *desertio*, which means "to leave, abandon, forsake."

In this context, I use *desertion* to refer to situations where A withdraws from B and refrains from the legitimate and necessary confrontation. That this desertion might be caused by A's fear of intimizing B is no excuse. Desertion always fails the fundamental pedagogical responsibility of wanting to influence and pay attention to others.

On this basis, the concept can be defined as follows:

Desertion: When a person who carries a pedagogical responsibility refrains from influencing those he or she is responsible for, or refrains from encountering the individual through a necessary and legitimate confrontation.

Desertion can be illustrated like this:

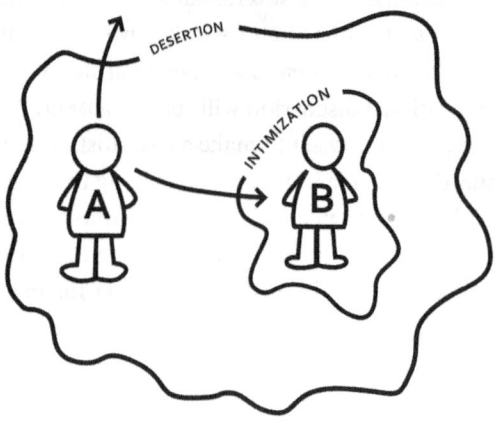

Fig. 2

CONFRONTATION

Another central finding in the interviews was the informants called for more teachers who wanted to influence their students— teachers who had the courage to challenge their students, and who genuinely wanted to affect them—without intimization. In short, they called for teachers who dared to come close to their students, without coming too close. We can call this "coming close" *confrontation*, and it can be defined as follows:

> **Confrontation**: When a person who carries a pedagogical responsibility influences another person in a constructive and legitimate manner through mature conversation, authority, knowledge, and involvement, all serving the well-being of the other person.

In other words, confrontation is a form of involvement where A comes close to B because A estimates this is in B's best interest. A might be noticing some unrealized needs for knowledge or guidance that B is not aware of. A is then able to challenge B through personal questions, but because the foundation of their relationship is trust, B does not experience it as an intimization.

It is likely the confrontation is still tied to an experience of discomfort, but in the long run B experiences the encounter as something *good*. In fact, never experiencing such healthy and constructive confrontation from people who want to influence our lives can have catastrophic consequences. No one can develop in a healthy manner without facing confrontation.

Therefore, I maintain a clear distinction between intimization as a negative concept and confrontation as a positive concept. Nevertheless, it can be difficult in practice to determine whether we are facing an example of intimization or confrontation. Therefore, the aim of making this distinction is not to learn how to single out the sinners, but to increase *everyone's* attention, caution and ethical awareness.

WITHDRAWAL

Just like our need for healthy confrontations, we also have a fundamental need for the opposite, namely, that those who influence us withdraw and leave us in peace. This need for A to pull pack is often crucial in the wake of a confrontation. I refer to this as *withdrawal*. To the child, this can find expression in a need for the adult to withdraw in order to allow the child to attend his or her own activities, thoughts, and feelings undisturbed.

In the case of desertion, we are dealing with an attempt to escape; you run away, and thereby you let the other person down. In the case of withdrawal, the pullback is a *necessity*—an act of consideration and care.

When an adult encounters a child, either at home, at school or in a day care institution, the adult can sometimes be in a position of powerlessness. His only option is then to withdraw, as his state of powerlessness might bring him to commit an offense against the child. Such a withdrawal can be a somewhat shocking experience to the child, but combined with the fact that the child gets to be in peace, it often brings out a more constructive pattern of behavior in the child.

Besides being careful in making sure confrontation does not merge into intimization, we must also be sure our withdrawals do not turn into desertions, where a state of anger or helplessness leads us to fail the other person.

Despite this potential danger, I strongly believe children today have a significant need to be in peace—from overprotective educators and worried parents with good intentions—not to mention the modern ball-and-chain known as the smartphone. It is important the child is allowed to freely experience and try things out without a feeling of constant surveillance. Children have a fundamentally need for adults to be able to withdraw.

On this basis, withdrawal can be defined as follows:

Withdrawal: When a person who carries a pedagogical responsibility, due to necessity, withdraws from the other person in a constructive, legitimate, and time-limited manner that serves the well-being of the other person.

When we add *confrontation* and *withdrawal* to the model, it looks like this:

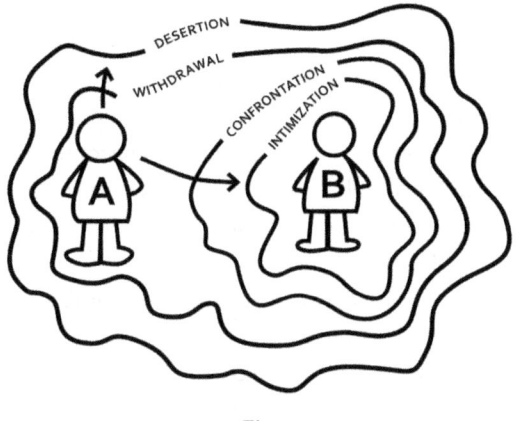

Fig. 3

At the center of the illustration, we find B, who can be either a child, student, listener, or something completely different. For the person who carries the pedagogical responsibility (A), the point of departure is halfway between the center and the periphery of the model, and from here he or she has the opportunity to move either toward or away from B.

Closest to B, we find the limit of *intimization*, which A should never overstep. Notice the distance between B and this limit is not static. In some situations, A can get rather close to B and still avoid intimization. However, B's personal limit varies, and sometimes A must keep a greater distance from B to avoid intimization. For example, ten-year-old Sophie can deal with her teacher telling her off but she is more sensitive when her teacher pushes her on religious issues.

What makes this a delicate balance is every human being has an individual limit of intimization which changes over time. This applies to all four limits in figure 3 in that they are neither inborn, eternal, objective, nor unchangeable. Fundamentally, they are all acquired, culture-specific, subjective, and changeable, but they exist in every individual.

Outside the limit of intimization, we find the limit of *confrontation*. This is the limit that A ought to cross now and then in order to respond to B's need for confrontation. Perhaps a five-year-old needs to be told clearly that biting others is not acceptable. To a third-grader, it can be a matter of understanding that tomorrow you *must* remember to bring your library book to school. To a group of teenagers in a Christian youth group, it can be about encountering a strong and firm challenge to become a follower of Jesus. And to a crowd of listeners at a church service, the confrontation can take place through a strong, personal communication of the forgiveness of sin through Jesus Christ.

I refer to the zone between the limit of intimization and the limit of confrontation as the *zone of confrontation*. Those who hold the pedagogical responsibility should never be permanently situated in this zone, but *when* they are in it, they must be both frank and cautious at the same time. They must be frank, knowing they can benefit others by confronting them, and they must be cautious, knowing in this zone they are moving closer to the limit of intimization.

Furthest from the center, we find the limit of desertion, which is the limit A should not cross, as this leads to a neglect of B, who is then left behind without the degree of involvement he or she is entitled to. This line is not stable either. In some areas, A can pull back quite far without B feeling abandoned. In other areas, B needs A to remain closer in order to not feel let down. This gets complicated further by the fact we all have our individual limitations in terms of when we feel deserted. This individual limit also tends to change over time.

A bit closer to the center, we find the limit of *withdrawal*, which A ought to cross now and then—either as self-protection or out of consideration for B. I refer to the zone between the limit of withdrawal and the limit of desertion as the *zone of withdrawal*. Those who hold the pedagogical responsibility should not be permanently situated in this zone, but *when* they are in it they must simultaneously be frank and cautious. They must be frank, knowing they can benefit others by withdrawing from them, and they must be cautious, knowing in this zone they are getting closer to the limit of desertion.

Let me give a few examples. At home, the five-year-old has a need for his parents to stop making rules about *everything* and constantly intervening with his activities. The third-graders also need to encounter their teacher's forgiveness, understanding, and willingness to compromise. The teenagers in the youth group should not only experience a challenging and serious tone from the adult leaders, they must also encounter a fun, laid-back, and friendly atmosphere. In the Sunday sermon, the congregation should not only be met by an emotional and personal testimony; sometimes a more analytical and objective message is equally uplifting.

NEGLECT, RESPECT, AND OUR EVERYDAY ZONE

At first, we might see intimization and desertion as two ends on a continuum, as shown in figure 4.

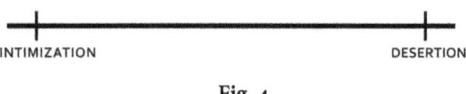

Fig. 4

However, I believe we reach a more realistic picture by bending the line, letting the two ends lean toward one another, as illustrated in figure 5.

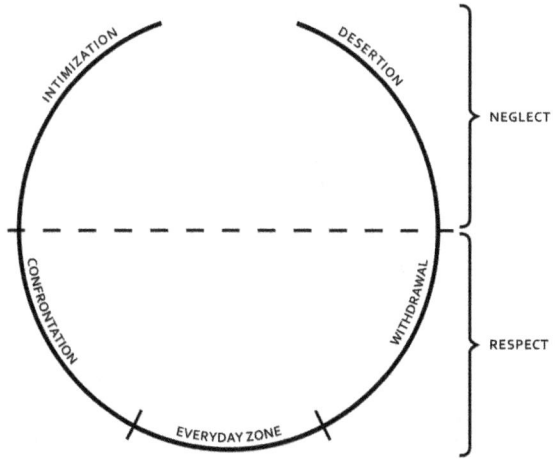

Fig. 5

Intimization and desertion are rather similar concepts, and fundamentally their source of origin might in fact be the exact same, namely, neglect. Therefore, it is more to the point to place them next to each other, as in figure 5, rather than at each end of a continuum.

Even though this is only a model, this modification allows us to draw a horizontal line across the circle. This line marks the boundary between *neglect*, which characterizes the influence described by the concepts above the line, and *respect*, which characterizes the influence described by the concepts below the line. Thus, this analysis provides us with two words that can replace our hitherto-less-precise discussion of "positive influence" versus "negative influence."

Negative influence is characterized by *neglect*.

Positive influence is characterized by *respect*.

Intimization takes place when there is a lack of distance, and when A does not *respect* that B is an independent individual with individual rights. Desertion takes place when the distance is too great and A does not *respect* B as a fellow human being who deserves a part in A's understanding of a good, true, and beautiful life.

Between the limit of desertion and the limit of confrontation we find a zone I refer to as the "everyday zone of influence." This is where the bulk of the upbringing and education unfolds, and it is a rather conflict-free space, separate from the zones of confrontation and withdrawal. However, this does not mean A can navigate unconsciously within it for an extended period of time. Sudden and unforeseen situations tend to arise which necessitate A stepping into the zone of confrontation or withdrawal, and then the risk of intimization or desertion arises.

In the following sections, I will describe in greater detail the nature of these various limits and zones. But before I do so, I want to emphasize that *mutual trust* between A and B, which is absolutely crucial to all upbringing, education, and ministry, can only be established within the three intermediate zones when both A and B are able to move smoothly between them. On the other hand, mutual *mistrust* between A and B arises when we move inside the limit of intimization and outside the limit of desertion. Therefore, it is crucial to forge an awareness and caution in both A and B regarding the importance of these zones and limits. The legitimacy and utility of our upbringing, education, and ministry depend on it.

The weakness of the model is it presents B as passive, while A plays the active part. This does not correspond with reality, where A's actions in relation to B are formed through interaction with B. This is true regardless of whether B is a child or an adult, but when B is an adult, certain special circumstances come into play.

WHEN B IS AN ADULT

The model assumes A is almost always an adult, but naturally there will be situations where A is below the age of majority. This can be the case when older siblings look after their younger siblings, or when dealing with young volunteers. In these situations, the psychology described here also applies, although the level of responsibility deviates a bit. This being said, the model assumes A to be an adult. However, it makes a significant difference whether or not B is an adult.

When B is an adult, he or she carries a larger part of the responsibility for making sure the influencing is conducted in a respectful manner. Naturally, the child also carries a certain responsibility toward the adult—but the younger the child the smaller the responsibility. But when B comes of age, the level of responsibility changes, both in practice and in principle.

To give an example, this applies in the relationship between preacher and listener. In this relationship, the adult listener must often exert some degree of self-protection. If, for instance, a certain preacher makes you feel claustrophobic or distressed, then maybe you should stop listening to that preacher, at least for a while. However, the opposite scenario is often the case—namely, the listener lacks the independence and resources required to keep the preacher at a proper distance.

Although the adult listener carries a larger responsibility than the child when it comes to allowing the influence of a preacher, the preacher also carries a significant responsibility. This is true because some people can still be immature and vulnerable despite having turned eighteen, and because some of the same unhealthy mechanisms can be activated when a preacher intimizes or deserts an adult.

OUR INDIVIDUAL DIFFERENCES

We are all different. No parents, teachers, or preachers are the same, and we all carry individual strengths and weaknesses. In the context of influencing, this means some are more inclined to intimize others, while they are also best at confronting. Others tend to lean toward desertion, but are also better at withdrawing than others. In general, these predispositions are highly determined by our personalities.

In a family, the father might have a personality that often, and sometimes too often, confronts the children with their duties or the family rules, while the mother is better at sensing the current mood and individual needs of the children. She then becomes the one who works toward compromise in the family, and who takes responsibility for making the necessary exceptions from the family rules.

Something similar is often true regarding the employees in a kindergarten, schoolteachers, or youth ministry leaders.

The point isn't that we should not challenge each other. Especially if a dominant individual attempts to pull everyone in his or her direction—either toward confrontation or withdrawal. In such situations, it is often necessary to draw a clear line and emphasize the value and legitimacy of various approaches and the need for mutual respect.

The secret is to learn how to warn each other against mistakes and biases when moving in the space of influence, while also being able to appreciate diversity and see the value of individual differences.

THE RESPONSIBILITY OF THE GROUP AND THE ENVIRONMENT

In real life, B is rarely constituted by a single individual. In most cases, B is a *group* of people, such as the children in a kindergarten, the students in a classroom, a group of children at church, or the members of an audience.

Therefore, the final model ought to look like this, where B is represented as a group, and where the grey area shows the zone for influence with respect:

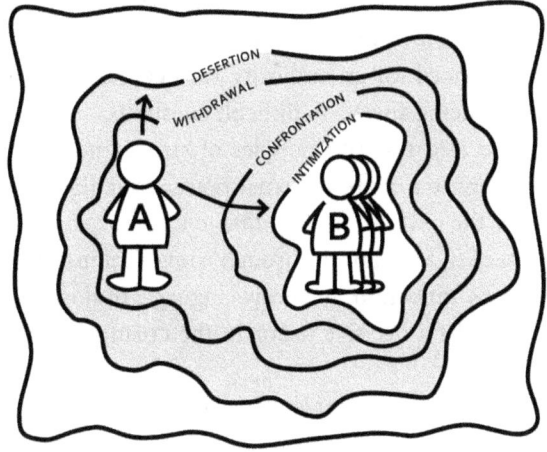

Fig. 6

This modification is significant as it draws attention to the importance of group dynamics in the context of influence. Some group dynamics make the group feel less responsible, or otherwise responsible, as opposed to the individual.

Due to group-psychological mechanisms, B can either choose to be seduced along with the rest of the group or to object to an intimizing or deserting teacher, preacher, or leader. The second option, however, does not remove the responsibility of the individual in relation to the collective behavior of the group.

The problems of intimization and desertion can also arise because the group (B)—or a certain environment such as a church—ascribes too much individual importance to A. Their expectations are too high and thus unrealistic. An indicator of this tendency is when A comes to be seen as an expert not only within his or her own field but in all other areas as well. If he is a gifted preacher, the group (B) also elects him to be a skilled leader. But this is often a mistake.

Often, it can be B's own insecurity or indolence that sparks these unrealistic expectations toward A. Such expectations can be difficult for A to keep at bay, as they often appeal to A's own need for confirmation. However, they can also be caused by B's fundamental human need for an authority who can always provide a clear and convincing answer to difficult questions.

There are also several examples of strong individuals who manage to exercise a more informal power over the others in a group. Under the cover of *not wanting to exercise power,* they exercise a form of hidden power through conversations, slandering, strategic silence, innuendo, and body language. In this way, strong individuals can be a decisive factor in the creation of unhealthy group dynamics.

Another central mechanism is the so called "halo-effect," which is triggered when a person does something extraordinary and therefore comes to enjoy an unreasonable degree of tolerance within the group. This tolerance allows him or her to get away with things no one else would. The remaining group members lower their guard and cease to challenge A.

A DISTINCT PROBLEM WITHIN THE CHURCH?

Within the church, there is often a request for strong, visionary preachers and spiritual leaders. In fact, it is likely this demand has increased in recent years due to the complexity of the modern world, the growing stream of information, and the lack of time to process it all. Under such circumstances, having a strong individual to follow can be an advantage.

The demand for strong leaders might also be growing due to an exaggerated democratism within the church. Today, everyone should have a say in every matter, and no one can be an authority in any respect. No one should be seen as more experienced or more authoritative than anyone else. In communities marked by such a misunderstood anxiety in relation to spiritual leadership, a growing request for a dominating leader is partly self-inflicted.

In addition, the need for strong, visionary Christian leaders often grows bigger because the gap between the Christian subcultures and the secular majority increases. The ordinary Christian, therefore, needs a spiritual teacher and leader who can provide an answer to every issue. The leader is placed in a position from which he must connect two separate cultures. In other words, the leader becomes a gatekeeper who must guarantee those within the subculture are on the right track.

Such tendencies are almost impossible to avoid, and they might just be a precondition when Christian communities become minorities. However, we should still do our utmost to be critically aware of these mechanisms.

The analysis provided above implies the risk of fostering preachers and leaders who are unable to influence with respect is greatest in relatively small and homogeneous communities. In fact, the subculture might be directly dependent on such preachers and leaders. This state of affairs can make it increasingly difficult for the spiritual leader, as well as the ordinary person, to see what is at stake in his or her own community. As professor Niels Gunder Hansen puts it, "It is obviously difficult to see the sect when it fills our entire reality."[1]

If Christian communities become too small, and their members come to agree too much, this can lead to an unhealthy relationship between A and B. The same thing can happen when a Christian group loses its connection to other communities and is no longer challenged by other external ideas.

In all of this, it can be difficult to distinguish between cause and effect. Is it the small, homogeneous communities that generate

---

1. Hansen, *Lille dreng med rejseskrivemaskine*, 129.

intimizing and deserting leaders and preachers, or is it the other way around? But perhaps this question is a minor issue as they are probably just two sides of the same coin. Regardless, this tendency should make us question how small faith-based communities can become without becoming unhealthy. And, if we are currently a part of a small community ourselves, we should be aware of the mechanisms mentioned above.

In order to avoid such unhealthy dynamics between preacher and listener in a church community, the listeners should, among other things, lower their expectations of the preacher while also exercising greater tolerance and patience toward him or her. These two disciplines are interconnected. If one has lower and more realistic expectations of the preacher, it becomes easier to be tolerant and patient. If the expectations are too high, the listener easily becomes impatient and tends to judge the preacher more severely.

In addition, it should be mentioned this (unhealthy) call for strong leaders is not only found within the church. We also see a strong request for significant leaders in secular youth cultures, where everything is allowed, and where it is hard to find new boundaries to break.

THINKING AND ACTING

It is my hope the model presented in this chapter can be a help to those who carry a pedagogical responsibility. It is absolutely necessary that individuals who influence others are repeatedly reminded of the responsibility they carry, and of the ditches and pitfalls that run along the road upon which they travel.

Nonetheless, the crucial point is of course to not only use this model to *think* more clearly about the subject, but to use it to become better prepared and equipped in order to *act* more appropriately. To act more appropriately does not mean to act flawlessly, as no one is ever perfect when it comes to parenthood, teaching, or preaching. To some extent, we all find ourselves in a grey area on these matters, but if the model can guide those who carry a pedagogical responsibility in the right direction—making them a bit better at influencing with respect—then we have come a long way.

It is my assessment that society today faces a strong need to learn how to confront others in a positive manner, meaning with respect. This challenge will be further addressed in the following chapter.

Chapter 3

FURTHER PERSPECTIVES ON INTIMIZATION, DESERTION, CONFRONTATION, AND WITHDRAWAL

THERE IS STILL A lot more to say about the four concepts presented in the model in chapter 2. Therefore, this chapter goes into further detail by discussing four relevant examples—one for each concept in the model.

AN EXAMPLE OF INTIMIZATION

The Norwegian film *The Other Side of Sunday* (1996) tells the story of a girl, Maria, whose father is a pastor. The film portrays Maria's struggle with the powerful influence that confronts her at home and in her father's church.

Maria's father is emotionally distanced from his children, as his actions and attitudes are fully dictated by his religious principles. Throughout the film, this combination of insensibility and strict influencing becomes a central element in the intimization that Maria and her siblings experience.

In the beginning, Maria longs to experience her father's acceptance and empathy, but in vain. Instead, all she encounters is her father's dogmatically correct Christian views and opinions. The film portrays a father who does not see his child. The father focuses on his children's obedience and fails to respect his children as independent individuals. Maria reacts to this neglect through a combination of grief and anger.

In general, the film portrays a range of adults who, in various ways, abuse their power and authority to illegitimately access the conscience of their children. This becomes clear in a scene where the father tells Maria, "Ask forgiveness for your sins!" This violent attack on his daughter's conscience, through which the father attempts to control her religious life, leads to the opposite outcome, namely Maria's wish not to publicly confirm her Christian faith in church.

A central element in the intimization portrayed in *The Other Side of Sunday* is the untrustworthiness the father represents. He preaches about joy in the church, but he never expresses any joy himself. He reacts aggressively toward Maria's growing sexuality while he himself has had a secret relationship with a female employee. This discrepancy between words and actions is a central reason why Maria experiences her father as intimizing.

Something similar is true for another character in the film, a youth minister who also puts spiritual pressure on Maria and her peers, but who, when he gets the chance to be alone with her, attempts to kiss her. He immediately regrets his actions and tells her she must use her beauty to serve Jesus. Maria is disappointed by his inability to express his feelings, and she despises his indecisiveness. As with the father, the youth minister lacks coherence between words and actions. He is neither true to his religious convictions nor to his emotional longings.

Thus, another central mechanism of intimization is revealed, namely, intimization is often fueled either by a lack of contact with one's own emotions, or by a lack of control over one's own emotions. In their attempt to influence Maria, both the father and the youth minister overstep her boundaries. In both cases, the transgression is an attempt to cover up a hidden aspect of their own lives, namely, they both carry with them intense and often sexual emotions. This emotional repression leads to lies and dishonesty, which undermine their credibility and lead to a growing need for exerting authoritative control over others.

From a Christian perspective, *The Other Side of Sunday* portrays the danger of using God's name as a means for intimization. It illustrates how influence becomes extra potent when it is not only exerted by an adult but also by a god who, to the receiver, becomes indistinguishable from the adult.

WHAT CHARACTERIZES INTIMIZATION?

From interviews, research and film, we can identify a range of distinctive features that characterize intimization:

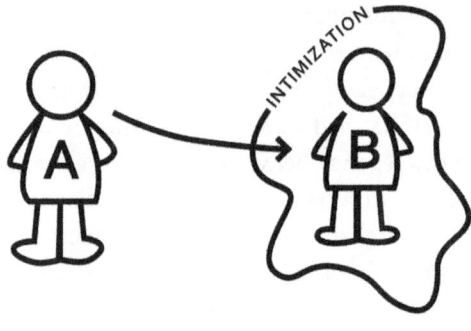

Fig. 1

The approach to other people and their opinions

- B is overisolated from other ideologies and opinions.
- A sets up strong and simplified enemy images.
- B's freedom to resist A's influence is strongly limited.

The intimizing atmosphere

- Insecurity.
- Distrust and calculation.
- B's own thoughts, feelings and will are set aside.

Intimizing forms of communication

- Indirect and insinuating communication that avoids real confrontation.
- The influence and opinions are stuffed down B's throat.
- B is the object, not the subject, of A's communication of truth and principles.

The methods of intimization

- A takes advantage of B's fear of not being loved or respected.
- A talks too much and rarely listens.
- A often checks to make sure B has the right opinions, i.e., the same as those of A.

The intimizing personality

- Insecurity leads to authoritarian behavior.
- A discrepancy between words and actions.
- A lack of contact with one's own inner life. Suppression of emotions.

The person who is being intimized feels . . .

- shameful (I am not as I should be) vs healthy, a concrete sense of guilt.
- condemned and inferior.
- encircled and trapped.

The person who is being intimized can develop the following character traits:

- Immaturity and a lack of self-reliance.

- Narcissistic features leaning toward either depression or exaggerated self-importance.
- A reduced ability to think freely and rationally.

WILL INTIMIZATION LAST FOREVER?

It is a striking fact that those who have been victims of intimization generally do not pass on to others the opinions that were forced on them. The degree of dissociation varies, but almost all these individuals feel a need to remove themselves noticeably from their past. This behavior seems to indicate the effect of intimization has a limited time span.

This tendency toward dissociation does not mean those who have experienced intimization within a Christian context leave their faith behind—but neither do they fully adopt the convictions they were taught earlier in life.

This observation leaves us with a thought-provoking and contradictory state of affairs, namely, those who are most zealous in their attempt to influence generally do not reach their goal. At least the result is often a division among their receivers into two groups—one that follows them blindly and one that rebels.

Although there is no fixed formula that ensures a certain outcome from a certain influence, there are indications that influence accompanied by an articulated freedom to either accept or reject is far more durable and solid.

AN EXAMPLE OF DESERTION

The Other Side of Sunday also contains examples of desertion. Maria's mother, who is mentally ill, is highly absent in the life of her daughter, who is only a teenager. This is partly due to her mental condition, but it is as much due to an act of desertion. Maria's mother never stands up for her daughter when she faces the father's intimization. She always sides with her husband, and generally she is portrayed as a bleak and suppressed individual who, due to her own submission, is unable to show her daughter any personal affection.

However, the strongest example of desertion comes from Maria's father. In her father, Maria encounters intimization and desertion simultaneously. After overstepping her limits, he immediately abandons her in emotional isolation. Let me give three examples:

- Maria's father is morally inconsistent but is not receptive to Maria's criticism.
- He tries to force Maria to confess a sin but does not show any general interest in her inner life.
- When Maria asks him if he loves her, he avoids a personal answer and says a father always loves his children.

Throughout the film, we sense Maria's longing for her father. She wants to break through to him, but he keeps rejecting her. This insensitive nature, which he hides behind his correct behavior, is an expression of the father's desertion of his daughter.

WHAT CHARACTERIZES DESERTION?

When it comes to desertion, we can also identify certain distinctive features:

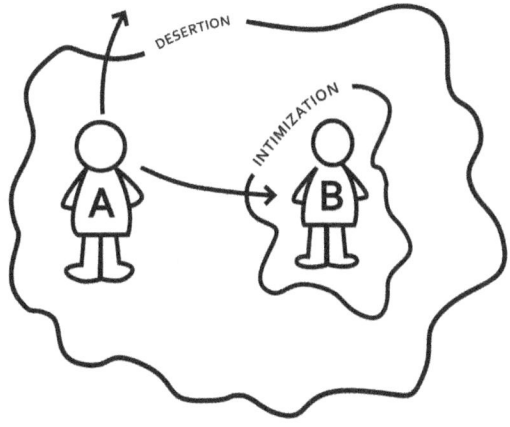

Fig. 2

The relationship between A and B

- A is silent about matters that are relevant to B, such as other people's opinions.
- A considers certain issues taboo, such as sex, death, suffering, and evil.
- A displays a lack of interest in B's thoughts and viewpoints.
- A does not take on the task of being B's lawyer and protector.

On a deeper level, this reveals that . . .

- A limits B's world instead of opening it up.
- A leaves B behind in a no-man's land.
- A lacks empathy and compassion.
- A approaches B through correct principles but lacks personal involvement.

A common denominator in these characteristics is A's unwillingness to be present in B's life. Respectful influence is a matter of being able to listen and show involvement and empathy. The absence of these qualities leads to desertion, which B often experiences as a form of betrayal.

AN EXAMPLE OF CONFRONTATION

I draw my example of confrontation from my interview survey.
Jeppe, who went to a Christian free school in Denmark:

> When we reached eighth grade, we had a new female teacher who really became a role model for me in many ways. Her vision and methods were clear from day one. From the first day, she would comment and correct every little mischief, and after six weeks, we could all relax because she had been clear and consistent from the start. We realized that school wasn't just about goofing around. This was a place for learning, and we all really liked her.

FURTHER PERSPECTIVES

[Interviewer]: "What characterizes the positive form of influence that wants to communicate something without intimizing?"

[Jeppe]: "It is characterized by the teacher's ability to listen to and be affected by the thoughts and opinions of his or her listeners, while at the same time being enthusiastic and fully engaged in the subject matter. . . . When experiencing this, you realize that the person trying to influence you is also willing to support you all the way through. If we think of this process as a journey, we are not meant to travel without a specific aim, or without a map to follow. We are not supposed to just power ahead in blinkers. It is about walking together and being willing to stop and change direction."[1]

WHAT CHARACTERIZES CONFRONTATION?

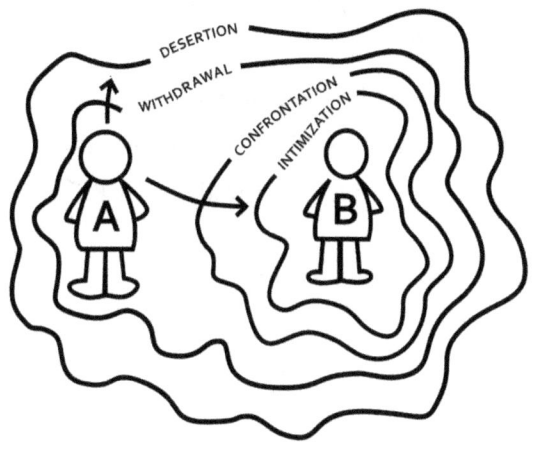

Fig. 3

Confrontation is characterized by A being:

- Consistent.
- Clear.

---

1. Pedersen, *Påvirkning med respekt*, 136–37.

- Caring.
- Empathic.

In addition, a person who confronts others must be willing to:

- break taboos.
- make reasonable demands.
- provide freedom within a safe environment.
- go beyond the exterior and ask about B's inner life.

It seems those who are able to respectfully confront others are often also capable of withdrawing at the right time, as confrontation is a matter of:

- finding a balance between listening and speaking.
- wanting something for B and walking alongside B.
- taking a stand while being ready to let B's opinions affect them.
- being fair and creating trust.

With regard to religious influence it seems to be important that faith:

- is an integral part of A's person.
- is visible in A's behavior and actions.
- is constructively and appropriately phrased.
- is expressed through a sincere interest and care in relation to B.

AN EXAMPLE OF WITHDRAWAL

My example of withdrawal also comes from the interview survey:

Bridget, who attended a Christian free school and a Christian boarding school:

[Interviewer:] "How do you influence someone in a positive way?"

[Bridget:] "By being clear—and by keeping a distance, I think. It is important that a teacher is able to master that balance. It can be difficult because some teachers might feel that they lose grip when they draw back. I recognize that feeling myself. I tend to think that I must be on top of things all the time, instead of saying, 'maybe I could learn something today.' When children feel that someone listens to them they also become more open to influence—if I should be a bit strategic about it. Because then they think: 'OK, she has listened to me, and the most important things have been said—then I must also accept the decision she makes.'"[2]

WHAT CHARACTERIZES WITHDRAWAL?

Withdrawal is characterized by:

- A realizing and admitting his or her own mistakes.
- A allowing B to grapple with difficult challenges.
- A encouraging B to act independently.
- A being open to questions, doubts, and dialogue.

Withdrawal is characterized by A refraining from:

- surveilling B.
- overprotecting B.
- taking a relevant responsibility away from B.
- having feelings and opinions on behalf of B.

---

2. Pedersen, *Påvirkning med respekt*, 143.

Withdrawal, combined with confrontation, can lead to:

- B learning to trust in his or her own abilities and opinions.
- B becoming independent.
- B getting in touch with his or her own thoughts and feelings.
- B developing a personal expression of his or her own faith or conviction.

It seems those who are able to withdraw when necessary are often also able to confront others in a timely manner, as withdrawal is a matter of:

- A being able to wait for B's own initiative and to support the process when necessary.
- A communicating clearly while challenging B to act independently.
- A getting involved while also leaving B in peace.
- A recognizing B while also wanting B to progress.

A NO-MAN'S LAND IS NOT AN OPTION

In both intimization and desertion, B is being let down by A, who either comes too close or draws too far back. If A withdraws too far, and for too long, he loses touch with B. If A comes too close to B, their perspectives become intermingled to such an extent that A can no longer tell his own needs from B's, which leads A to misuse B as a means to an end.

Thus, success in the field of upbringing, education, and preaching depends on one's ability to balance the need to be close to the other, thereby creating a healthy connection, with the need to maintain a distance to the other, which makes it possible for both parties to stay in touch with themselves.

When A is a schoolteacher, he or she ought to represent culture and society in the eyes of the student, while also representing the student in the eyes of culture and society. If the teacher succeeds at both, he or she combines confrontation with withdrawal.

However, we do not only influence through what we say, but also through what we choose *not* to say. Let us take an example from the field of religion. Some might claim we can avoid religious intimization by simply refraining from influencing others on religious matters or by doing it in a neutral manner. This might sound like an intriguing way of avoiding the pitfalls of influence. However, this path is not a possibility, as the absence of influence, or neutral influence, is also a form of influence.[3]

If, for instance, children never hear about God, or only hear about him when visiting church, they are merely brought up with a different idea of who God is. This idea will be different from the Christian understanding of God as a God who is not bound to a specific location. From this perspective, we cannot live for a single moment or have a single thought, or just look out the window, without God being a relevant constituent.

Even when we choose to talk about God in a neutral and informative manner, we still cannot avoid influencing our receivers. Apart from being rather boring and unengaging, this form of impersonal influence is also a conscious choice. It is a form of influence that moves the listener toward an unauthentic and purely intellectual image of God—an image that does not correspond with a Christian understanding.

In other words, desertion is also a form of influence. It is never a neutral position in the same way a soldier who deserts his army is never in a neutral position. By choosing to desert, the soldier influences the outcome of the war.

In human life, choosing no-man's-land is never an option. This is true for both children and adults, and it is a result of our fundamental nature as individually responsible beings. Because we live in a constant struggle between good and evil, it always takes an active effort to influence with respect.

---

3. For further clarification see Sandsmark, *Is World View Neutral Education Possible and Desirable?*

Chapter 4

THE IMPORTANCE OF CONFRONTATION

WITHIN A DANISH CONTEXT, it seems to me the risk of intimization, whether at home, in school, or in church, has declined in recent years, while the risk of desertion has grown. My international readers must assess whether this is the case in their region of the world as well. If this is the case, it is important we take a closer look at the positive features of confrontation.

INTIMIZATION IS MORE VISIBLE THAN DESERTION

One of the differences between intimization and desertion is the latter is usually harder to grasp than the former. A reason for this is intimization is usually *more visible* than desertion. The former is characterized by the *presence* of transgressive behavior, whereas the latter is characterized by the *absence* of positive confrontation, delimitation, and firmness. The presence of something negative is usually more visible than the absence of something positive.

In practical terms, we might say, once we gather the courage, it is usually easier to root out intimization than desertion in our lives. I have a childhood memory of a situation where my father not only confronted me, but intimized me. I acknowledged this a long time ago, and I forgave him. My point is once we become aware of such concrete acts of intimization they also become palpable, and therefore they are simpler to respond to than acts of desertion. Through such acknowledgments, we add strength to our independence and self-worth.

If my father had never expected anything from me or made any reasonable demands, it would have been far more difficult. It would have been far more complicated to respond to a father who always avoided confrontation.

When looking back on the preaching I experienced as a child, there were, as I see it, a number of preachers who used their position for intimization. This goes for preaching directed at children, teenagers, young adults, and grown-ups. I have listened to several so-called revival sermons and testimonies that took advantage of people's fear of condemnation, or that, even though the speaker was often unaware of it, made use of psychological methods to pressure the listeners into conversion.

This being said, I mainly experience a lack of healthy, confrontational preaching today, such as a clear and serious communication of the brevity of life, the certainty of death, and the scope of eternity, or a healthy call to personal repentance and conversion. Instead, I see a long line of preachers who are afraid to offend their listeners.

But the truth is the God of the Bible confronts us. We cannot approach him without having this experience. He does not always make sure we are healthy and fit, or we can find the car keys we lost last night. He is incomprehensible. He allows the most horrendous things to happen in this world, and our preaching has to acknowledge his wild and untamable nature. If we are raised with a faith that omits this side of God's nature, we often end up abandoning our faith when we suddenly encounter this reality in our own lives.

If we are not also familiar with these untamable aspects of his nature, we can never truly get to know God in his surprising goodness and overwhelming love. Today, when it comes to the sphere of preaching, I believe we cause more damage through desertion than through intimization. Therefore, I am willing to advocate the need for a new and respectful approach to confrontation through preaching. So, let us search for the positive potential hidden within the concept of confrontation (and withdrawal) when rooted in a foundation of mutual respect.

CONFRONTATION BASED ON THE REALITY OF ABSOLUTE TRUTH

Before I get to the positive potential of confrontation, I should mention confrontation is *a necessity*, whether or not we experience it as positive or negative. (A group or an individual can *experience* a confrontation as negative even though it is legitimate.)

Confrontation is both necessary and unavoidable because absolute truth exists. The existence of absolute truth is a consequence of the existence of God—not merely as a linguistic construction or a myth, but as an entity existing independently of human consciousness.

I am aware many will criticize the two propositions "absolute truth exists" and "God exists" for merely being empty statements or social constructions. I recognize this position, but at the same time I insist this approach is as much a subjective claim, conviction, or belief as my position is.

But when I maintain absolute truth exists, and God exists, it also becomes necessary to seriously consider the concept of confrontation. Confrontation is a natural consequence of the existence of something absolute. Of course I should emphasize none of us are able to concede the absolute truth or fully know the triune God. As human beings, we are limited and broken, and although God is not silent but speaks to us in multiple ways,[1] I do not hold the key that unlocks all the mysterious rooms in our lives.

Nor am I some sort of orthodox Muslim who believes he can obtain full insight into the will of Allah by following a specific imam who can interpret the Qur'an correctly on his behalf.

---

1. God speaks to us through creation, history, and our individual conscience. Although this communication is relatively blurred, it still comes from God. In addition, God speaks to us more clearly and directly through the Bible, which is inspired by him in a unique way. He speaks to us most clearly by entering our world through his son, Jesus Christ.

A significant part of human life is open and is not tied to an absolute truth. This is in accordance with God's intention. In these areas, truth is relative. This is the case in political issues, and it is the case when it comes to Christian upbringing. Several cultural issues are not tied to God's revelation. Instead, these are often defined through personal opinion and taste. To illustrate this point, we might think of a maritime fairway with buoys on both the starboard and port sides, as illustrated below.

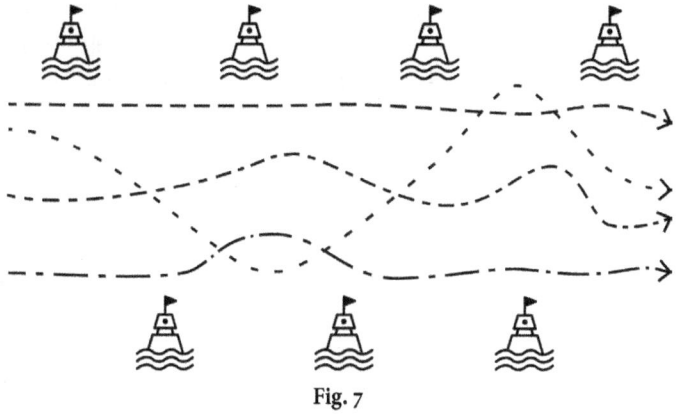

Fig. 7

God has not provided us with set norms in all areas of life. There are many things the Bible does *not* talk about. It first and foremost deals with the most important questions: Who is God? Who are we? What defines our relationship? How must we live?

God has honored us with the ability to make our own choices, for which we are personally responsible. God has placed buoys along the fairway of our lives—the most important one being the gospel of Jesus Christ and the revelation of him as our Savior and Lord. Other guiding principles are the Ten Commandments as interpreted by Jesus and the apostles in the New Testament. Within the framework of these buoys, which are expressions of absolute truth, we can move freely and in accordance with our own dreams and ambitions.

Those for whom we carry a pedagogical responsibility should not be given a complete manual for how to live their lives. On the contrary, we should support them in finding their own personal course. And as we guide them, we should also confront them with the fact there are some unavoidable buoys along the journey. We are obliged to point to theses buoys and speak truthfully about them. Not everything in life is floating freely. The most important reference points in life are firmly anchored to the ocean floor—and despite the fact no one can fully grasp the truth, we should always be frank and cheerful, knowing we are always close to God's will and truth when we stick to the course he has set for us.

Finally, it is important we never force anyone to stay within the buoys. The people we influence are always responsible for their own lives, and they are free to sail outside the buoys—and bear the consequences.

THE POSITIVE POTENTIAL OF CONFRONTATION

Again, let me emphasize confrontation holds positive potential when it is practiced in a balanced interplay with withdrawal. This is a fundamental premise in the central model presented here, and yet it is important we keep reminding ourselves of it. If we do not combine confrontation with withdrawal, the sphere of influence gets overheated. No one benefits from constant confrontation.

In addition, the confrontation loses its effect if it is not combined with withdrawal. When we experience an act of influence, it is important we are allowed a free and personal reaction. What we have encountered needs to be processed and adapted on a personal level. We need to examine and assess the input, and sometimes this demands long periods of withdrawal. This process is necessary in order for the confrontation to lead to a positive outcome.

If the person who carries the pedagogical responsibility is unable to balance confrontation with the necessary amount of withdrawal, the confrontation turns into intimization.

Now, allow me to mention four positive qualities of confrontation:

1. Independence

Most people will agree it is often through encounters with strong-minded people that we develop and mature as individuals. Independence does not spring from encounters with vague or dull individuals. Rather, it is born in encounters with people who want something for us, and whose drive to confront us is rooted in a sincere care for us.

This does not mean we take on *the same identity* or *the same opinions* as the person influencing us. Sometimes, the result is quite the opposite, and instead the person influencing us leads us toward the exact opposite opinion—or at least a modified version of his or her opinion.

This is often true when it comes to our *political standpoint*. A daughter often ends up with progressive viewpoints if her parents are conservatives, and vice versa. Naturally, it can be tough for the parents to acknowledge that their political influence on their child has led to the exact opposite outcome, nonetheless, the parents have helped their child reach independence through their influence.

In general, we might say healthy and legitimate influence is what forms our identity, and this formation is crucial in a time marked by great insecurity in relation to identity.

2. Coherence

Healthy confrontation creates coherence, at least in situations where the conveyed content is relatively consistent. I am not talking about a perfect system that answers all questions, but about a fundamental view of life. This can be a religious conviction, a political profile, or an ideological course. This form of consistent influence can provide a necessary coherence in the fragmented reality people of all ages experience.

Some have experienced that confrontation—or was it intimization?—forged a rejection of a consistent set of values with which they grew up, and this has led them to a state of uncertainty and insecurity. However, confrontation can also lead to the opposite outcome, which is a sense of *recognizability* and *safety*. This happens when the influencer's standpoints are coherent. This experience often relieves some of the pressure of always having to be original and innovative, as we step into a framework that reaches above and beyond the individual level.

3. Collective consciousness

In a time where the individual is more important than the collective, confrontation can help strengthen our collective consciousness. This is true because healthy confrontation presupposes something stands above our individual interests.

As an example, let us consider Christian norms and values. If we influence children and young adults with these norms and values, it naturally implies something stands above us all. There is something—in this case *God*—that defines a reality for all of us. Naturally, this form of influence can become constricting and unhealthy for the individual, but today there is a need to maintain the collective responsibility such norms and values create.

One of the negative consequences of individualism is loneliness. I might be master in my own house—but I also live there alone, and that makes me lonely. Although it might limit our individual freedom, a healthy confrontation with something that is true for all of us, and that we are obliged to, can diminish some of the loneliness that tends to surround us.

4. Healthy resilience

Generally, we have become more vulnerable during the last few decades. This is partly due to the growing sense of individuality in Western society. We have fewer people to lean on, and we experience an increasing number of broken human relations. All this adds to our vulnerability, which makes us more inclined to perceive ourselves as victims.

In the context of this book, this growing vulnerability leads to an enhanced attention to the issue of substantial influencing and verbal abuse and violations. When we place the individual on a pedestal, all forms of offense against it lead to a moral panic.

But, as a counterpoint to this panic, a healthy and respectful influence can provide us with a useful resilience that can help us stand up to those who speak against us. Of course we should never become insensitive to intimization or desertion, but we can only build thriving communities if we learn not to be too vulnerable. When individuals within a community are able to have diverse viewpoints and engage in a healthy discussion without intimization it provides a breeding ground for spiritual freedom and respect. This foundation tends to crumble if we are unable to deal constructively with intense, respectful influence.

CONFRONTATION AT HOME—UPBRINGING

Now and then, parents have to overstep the limit of confrontation in order to create a bearable atmosphere for everyone in the household. Let us take an example many will recognize. At dinnertime, a child refuses to put away the iPad, and the usual verbal instruction from the parents has no effect. In this situation, a reproaching confrontation can be a legitimate solution: "If you do not put down the iPad within two minutes, I'll take it from you." Usually, the child will experience this confrontation as negative and uncomfortable, but it is necessary, as the child, over time, needs to learn to master the technology that surrounds them, instead of being subjected to it.

At the same time, the parents must seek to understand the child as an equal human being who has their reasons for reacting as they do. For instance, they might acknowledge the child's right to disagree and become annoyed, while at the same time maintaining their initial position. This form of confrontation, when carried out in respect for the child, is a form of firm care that should not be labeled as intimization.

CONFRONTATION IN SCHOOL—TEACHING

Confrontation is also relevant in the context of education. Whether the subject is history or geography, the teacher always wants to convey something to the student, and it is crucial the student experiences this explicit intentionality in the teacher. This also means the teacher must make a visible effort to engage the students. Although they might not understand the purpose and value of the lesson at first, the teacher should rest assured he or she is doing the students a favor by confronting them with a subject matter that might be challenging to them.

The confrontation becomes even more vivid when the teaching deals directly with personal convictions, faith, and existential issues such as death. Here, the interplay between confrontation and withdrawal becomes essential. On the one hand, it is stimulating and healthy for the students to encounter teachers who hold strong personal beliefs and convictions, but on the other hand, the teacher must be extremely aware of the students' individual need to take their own stand. For instance, this balance is important when discussing and interpreting literature that deals with existential issues.

CONFRONTATION IN CHURCH—PREACHING

Christian preaching is one of the strongest forms of influence there is, because:

1. *Its content* is the word of God, which by nature is "living and active, sharper than any two-edged sword, piercing to the division of soul and of spirit, of joints and of marrow, and discerning the thoughts and intentions of the heart."[2]
2. God's Spirit is present and has promised to build and nourish our faith. In this space, people are brought into the kingdom of God.

---

2. Heb 4:12 (ESV).

3. Its form is personal engagement, direct appeal, challenges, and proclamation.

Here, it is important to stress the confrontation conducted through preaching is not primarily marked by a dull tone, but is fundamentally joyful. Or, to use the language of theology, confrontation with the gospel comes before confrontation with the law.

Today, a fundamental challenge within the church is to use *the form* of preaching to confront both children and adults with the gospel, i.e., to directly address, offer, and give away God's unconditional—or rather, Jesus-conditional—love and salvation. Today, many children, young adults, and grown-ups work hard to be good enough, cool enough, and popular enough, and to get as many likes as possible on various social media.

Today, we face a merciless tyranny that has become ingrained in our culture, media, and mentality. Its fundamental message is everything depends on you alone—having the perfect body, the highest grades, the best partner—and making sure you have a positive mindset and your identity and gender are constructed in accordance with your own emotions and beliefs.

Due to this tyranny, the gospel sometimes tends to become homeless within our churches. This happens when we start asking ourselves if we *believe* in the right way—when we turn our Christianity into a matter of personal effort—of building and upholding a decent religious life in order to please God.

When this happens, we need to be confronted with the gospel. We need to hear God has broken the wheel and lifted us into true freedom, that he invites us to rest in his strong hands because his Son has already done everything on our behalf.

And then, once this foundation has been set in stone, it is the preacher's job to confront the listeners with the more grave aspects of human life. These two elements are not mutually exclusive, and most of us experience this duality through the close relationships of marriage, parenthood, and friendship. Because my wife loves me, she is sometimes forced to confront me with my shortcomings. Because we love our children, we draw clear lines for them.

Because we love our friends, we address difficult and sensitive issues that threaten to suffocate our relationship.

It is healthy for us to be confronted with God's will, and it is an important task for all Christian preachers to communicate his will to listeners of all ages. It goes without saying that this must be done with great wisdom and empathy. It is not only a matter of articulating a theoretically correct message; it is a matter of doing it in a caring spirit because we believe human life is a serious matter.

THE INDIFFERENCE OF RELATIVISM AND THE NARROWNESS OF FANATICISM

Working with confrontation is always a matter of looking for the happy medium. This approach is supported by Norwegian writer Finn Egil Toennesen, who says:

> All upbringing involves a balancing act between two dangerous extremes. Life is so complex that it is impossible to give a detailed description of the happy medium. Every individual and every situation carry unique demands. In the sphere of influence, the two extremes are indoctrination as opposed to so-called neutrality. These two extremes are both characterized by a cold and impersonal attitude. Children need both openness and engagement. Therefore, we must seek to balance the indifference of relativism and the narrowness of fanaticism. It is often difficult to determine when an act of influence transgresses one of these limits. In practice, this judgement is based on subjective assessment and common sense. As in other areas of life, such boundaries can be difficult to pin down. It is as difficult as determining how much hair a person must lose before he can be defined as bald. Such definitions are always "hair-thin" and highly subtle. . . . The aim of upbringing is, strictly speaking, to help the child become a grown-up. From a physical perspective, we become grown-ups when we stop growing. However, the aim of upbringing is to foster *mature* individuals who are aware of their own limitations, and who have an open approach to their surroundings and

fellow human beings. According to Blaise Pascal, it is exactly this ability to acknowledge one's own limitations that reveals the greatness of man. Pascal argues that we can commit two fundamental errors in life. One is to reject reason and the other is to accept nothing apart from reason. Instead, we must embrace a faith that is open to the fundamental questions of life while also being tied to a fixed standpoint and a clear engagement.[3]

As *Christian* individuals who carry a responsibility in the areas of upbringing, education, and preaching, I believe we should consider these words carefully.

---

3. Tønnesen, *Verdier og livssyn i skole og barnehage,* 9–10, 116 (emphasis added).

Chapter 5

RELIGIOUS EXTREMISM

Since the terror attacks on September 11th, 2001, the Western world has been marked by an increasing focus on religious extremism, including phenomena such as:

- Radicalization
- Parallel societies
- Social control

The starting point was *Islamist* extremism, but the focus quickly turned toward *Christian* extremism as well. The common logic is if we must fight Islamist extremism, then it must be equally, if not more, relevant also to fight Christian extremism in the West—Christian extremists being those Christians who oppose such things as same-sex marriage and induced abortion. Even faithfulness toward the Bible is often categorized alongside the Salafist approach to the Qur'an.

A MATTER OF INFLUENCE

The connection between religious extremism and the field of *influence* is rather obvious, as religious extremism affects children, young people, and adults. If we apply the terminology presented in this book, then both Muslim and Christian extremists are accused of:

- *Intimization* through radicalization and severe social control.
- *Desertion* through the isolation of children and young adults from mainstream culture through parallel societies.

In Denmark, this debate has brought critical attention to religious private independent schools, which are now being regularly accused of intimization as well as desertion.

An important catalyst in the debate has been that several adults, especially of the younger generation, have stepped forward publicly with accusations against the Muslim and Christian environments in which they were raised.

Regardless if we find this increased focus on religious extremism uplifting or terrifying, it is an issue we all must take a stand on, also within the environments that stand accused—especially if we wish to influence with respect.

My insight into the Muslim communities is too limited for me to give an account of how the criticism is received in those communities. According to mainstream media, some Muslim communities are aware of the problem and are actively trying to minimize it, while other Muslim communities continue to promote religious extremism under the radar.

But is it true the church is a representative of religious extremism? Is it true that verbal abuse of children and young adults is taking place in Christian schools and in certain churches and Christian organizations?

As this book makes clear, there are examples of such abuse. Therefore, self-scrutiny within the church and other Christian communities is appropriate. However, the exact *magnitude* of religious extremism is still unknown, both historically and in the present day. As mentioned earlier, it is my impression this only occurs sporadically within the church today, and that desertion generally is a larger threat than intimization.

A proper investigation of the extent of religious extremism within the church, both historically and today, would be highly relevant—but first it is necessary to clearly define *the exact meaning of the term* "religious extremism," as this term still remains vague in the public debate. Too often, we define religious extremism by referring to its subject matter, although it ought to be defined through a consideration of its methods and forms.

The word "extremism" comes from the word "extreme," meaning *farthest removed from the ordinary or average*. Therefore, we must ask if it is the content or the methods that are out of the ordinary when speaking of religious extremism.

RELIGIOUS EXTREMISM SHOULD NOT BE DEFINED BY ITS CONTENT

Often times, the public debate defines everyone who holds extreme views as extremists, and extreme views are, per definition, those held by the minority. The majority is never extremist. Due to this public discourse, many will label you extremist if you, for instance, believe that sex belongs within the confines of marriage, that it is wrong for the church to marry two people of the same gender, or that death leads to either salvation or damnation.

Today, such beliefs are only applauded by a small minority in most Western countries, although only a few decades ago they were majority beliefs, or minority beliefs that were still generally respected. The problem in defining religious extremism by such categories of content is it labels all minorities as extremist by definition, and that is a dangerous path to go down.

In that case, both Nicolaus Copernicus (1473–1543) and Galieo Galilei (1564–1642) should be labled as religious extremists because their claim that the sun is the center of our solar system went against the beliefs of the religious majority at the time. From this perspective, Søren Kierkegaard (1813–1855) was an extremist as well—not in the field of science, but in the fields of theology, philosophy, ethics, and church politics, since he also represented a minority. One of his opponents, professor and bishop H. L. Martensen (1808–1884), would probably have labeled him an extremist had he been familiar with the term.

Let me give an example from recent history. The German pastor and resistance fighter Dietrich Bonhoeffer (1906–1945) was considered an extremist not only by the Nazi regime but also by the majority within the German church. He was executed only a few days before the fall of Nazi Germany, and the true value of his extremism was not recognized until after the war.

The problem of defining religious extremism by its content is the minority is sometimes right. Not only when it comes to the solar system, but also on ethical and faith-related issues. It is therefore an indispensable factor in a healthy democracy that it protects its minorities. Extreme viewpoints must be accepted as long as they are based on a well-informed and conscious foundation, and as long as they are not forced on anyone.

Therefore, the minority should not retreat into isolation. Rather, they should freely seek a dialogue with the majority, in the firm conviction that they have something to offer. This can be said to be the fundamental obligation of the minority.

RELIGIOUS EXTREMISM SHOULD BE DEFINED BY ITS METHODS

The definition of religious extremism should be based on a consideration of methods, means, and form. Extremism is revealed when violent methods are accepted; when convictions are forced on others; when the principles of democracy are put aside; or when participation in the public debate is refused. If Christian groups promote such methods, they deserve to be labeled as extremist.

However, it is misleading to categorize violent Islamists who support the Caliphate along with democratic Christians who speak out against same-sex marriage.

Let us consider another example. What made the left-wing groups of the seventies and eighties, such as the Baader-Meinhof Group, extremist was not their radical political *ideas*, but their radical political *methods*. Robberies, kidnapping, and murder were some of the most popular tools in their political toolbox.

Although necessary, it is not always easy to distinguish between content and method, as some political and religious ideologies are inextricably tied to the use of violence, force, and abuse. We might say the methods are sometimes embedded in the content. When this happens in a democratic context, society must demand those extremist content-elements be removed in order for that religious or political group to be accepted and protected within the democratic system.

Historically, this was the case in some left-wing movements, and it is the case in some Muslim communities today. Having learned from past mistakes, Muslims now face a crucial challenge in getting rid of the extremist potential, meaning certain methods within Islam, if they want to continue to enjoy the democratic protection of the minority.

Within the Christian church, we also find alarming traces of extremist methods. Consider, for instance, the Thirty Years' War (1618–48), not to mention the many cases of sexual abuse within the Catholic Church. Also, within the Protestant Church, we find unfortunate examples. However, there is a significant gap between these violations and the claim that all who hold certain views concerning sexual ethics or life after death are to be seen as extremists.

To sum up, you are not an extremist because you oppose free abortion, but you are if you throw Molotov cocktails at abortion clinics or assault doctors who perform abortions. You are neither extremist nor homophobic if you believe Christian churches should not offer to marry homosexual couples and refuse to do so, but you are if you despise and mock others due to their sexual orientation.

There *is* a risk that small, enclosed communities turn toward extremist methods, and I have provided examples of such instances above. If this reaches a point where members of such communities violate penal law, then the system of justice must take over. However, as long as no legal violations are taking place, it is not the job of the public authorities to define the line between legitimate confrontation and illegitimate intimidation. Should the authorities attempt to do so, perhaps as a misguided attempt to protect the children, it will lead to social control, thought-policing, and conscience interference, which is the opposite of spiritual freedom.

Nonetheless, this also means the individual Christian home, church, or school carries a crucial responsibility of educating and equipping parents, pastors, and teachers to teach, influence, and preach in a healthy and legitimate way, and especially in our time to step into positive confrontations.

RADICALIZATION

In recent years, the word *radicalization* has been used frequently, and has moved from the context of Islam to that of Christianity. It is primarily used to describe the process of children and young people who, through interaction with religious authorities, become radical.

However, being radical is not a dangerous thing in itself. This becomes evident when we consider the origin of the word. The word "radical" stems from the Latin word *radix*, meaning *root*. Thus, *radical* means "pertaining to the root of a cause; fundamental, inherent, thorough." Thus, *practicing radical charity* or *radically opposing violence* are positive traits.

On the other hand, we can rightly accuse our society of radical consumerism. For instance, I personally find it legitimate to be radical in criticizing the fact that printers, shoes, and other commercial products are deliberately produced to wear out fast.

Many adults also applaud a radicalization of the younger generation when it comes to their environmental consciousness, such as their awareness of the extreme amounts of plastic that fill the oceans and destroy life for plants, animals, and humans.

Radicalization in the negative sense is not a matter of being different or out of the ordinary. Negative radicalization arises when we begin to apply methods of isolation and indoctrination.

As an example, we might mention the echo chambers of social media as a current threat in relation to growing radicalization. In these online forums, we interact with people who share our views and opinions. Along with being like-minded, we can criticize and discredit our common enemies, whether they are Muslims, Conservative Christians, or fans of a football rival. It should of course be added that social media can also be used for the opposite purpose, as a healthy platform for encountering opposing viewpoints.

Today, the danger of radicalization in small Christian communities has dropped due to the increasing exposure to information through TV and other digital media. However, this also means parents in such communities must make an increasingly active effort to support their children, teenagers, and young adults, to ensure they experience a sincere interaction with thoughts and ideas that are not mainstream.

Influencing with respect is about holding clear and significant views *while* working to prevent isolation and indoctrination. And what good reasons are there really to seek isolation when you are truly convinced your beliefs and ethics are the most truthful?

This question naturally leads us to the issue of parallel societies.

PARALLEL SOCIETIES

In the West, the term *parallel society* is often used to describe somewhat isolated, urban ghetto areas dominated by a majority of Muslims. Usually, many of the residents in these areas barely speak the national language, and the unemployment rate is high. In addition, some areas are characterized by sharia-inspired parallel legal systems.

From here, the concept has been adopted into a Christian context and is now also used to describe Christian minorities who, for instance, hold restrictive views on alcohol consumption and sexual practices. To some extent, being considered a subculture or parallel society is a precondition religious minorities must tolerate. This is not problematic or dangerous in itself, although it can be tiring.

However, the term is rarely used in its pure form. Instead, it usually carries negative connotations that make us associate the idea of parallel societies with a resistance toward free, public debate and a general exclusivity in relation to the surrounding society. If we begin with a bit of self-criticism, we must admit a large portion of the responsibility for these connotations lies with those minorities who make a virtue out of interacting as little as possible with the surrounding community.

However, I do believe that the minorities, especially Christian minorities, I am most familiar with do their utmost to enter into debate with other minorities and with the majority. In general, our activities ought to be characterized by transparency. Faith and its various manifestations do not belong behind closed curtains or inside exclusive communities. It belongs in the public sphere and in houses that are fully open to the surrounding world.

The key is for subcultures to consider themselves as valuable countercultures in society. If minorities become defensive and shut themselves up, they end up strengthening the general perception that they seek to be isolated, parallel societies. Christian minorities should primarily be outgoing, rather than defensive, knowing they have a valuable contribution to make in an increasingly secular and pluralistic world. In everyday life this means the parents in such communities must encourage their children to join the local sports club or make friends with the other kids in the local community.

Here, the critical point lies in the choice between a strategy of protection and a strategy of preparation in the upbringing of our children. Naturally, there are elements within mainstream culture, language, and morality that our children, especially the youngest, must be shielded from, or at least gradually introduced to. This is both legitimate and necessary. But the important thing is to help them carry their Christian faith into various secular and pluralistic contexts. This becomes increasingly important as the children grow older.

Parents and children in Christian communities have a well-founded reason to believe their contribution to mainstream culture is both positive and invigorating. This is also the case in relation to questions of sexual morality and life after death. In fact, this point was made in 1888, when Norwegian bishop Heuch said the following:

> Shielding ourselves or our children from contact with the materialistic profanity of our time is impossible. Here, spiritual isolation is not an option. The spirit of this age is so permeated by the infectious agent of disbelief that to avoid breathing it in we would have to live in another era. . . . Our hope of rescue is not found in escape but in preparing to meet the approaching danger, in understanding the nature of this profanity, and in fighting it. Especially, I want to point out the necessity of teaching our children to recognize disbelief from a position of belief, before the world teaches them to recognize belief from a position of disbelief.[1]

SOCIAL CONTROL

Today, *social control* has become a central issue in the debate about influence within religious environments. Social control takes place when the community exerts a high degree of control to make sure the actions and opinions of the individual are in accordance with the norms of the community/sect. If a member of the community, especially a child or a young adult, steps outside the norms, they are punished—either through verbal correction or through threats of exclusion from the community. This punishment is often accompanied by threats of divine punishment or damnation.

However, social control is a wide concept that stretches from the mild forms that exist within any type of community to the harsher forms characterized by crude and offensive constraints and stigmatization of those who make just a tiny slip.

So, let us begin by emphasizing social control can be both necessary and productive. Any community needs a set of written and unwritten ground rules—from rules about what side of the road to drive on to the fact that socialist parties do not celebrate liberal ideas. Or, from the unwritten rule that the Johnsons go to

---

1. Horten, "Udsigt over Ungdomsskolens udvikling," 85.

church every Sunday to the undisputed fact that the members of an atheist society do not believe in God.

Along with such clearly defined communities comes an unavoidable need for the opportunity to react to deviations and carry out reprisals. You can exclude a member from a political party if he or she misbehaves, and those individuals who choose to break the norms of a community must accept some degree of exclusion. If a teenage son refuses to come to church, he cannot be forced, but he will have to accept the fact his decision hurts his parents.

Getting rid of all social control would mean getting rid of all communities—from our families to our local associations. Instead, we would be left in a world of lonely, uncommitted individuals who only had irregular and superficial contact with other people. In that sense, social control can be a gift. For instance, it is a good thing we perform social control regarding the drinking habits of our children or in order to reduce harassment in the work place.

Despite the positive aspects of social control, it is obvious we should be free to decide whether or not we want to be part of an ideological, religious or political community. However, the same freedom cannot be granted when it comes to being part of a nation-state. In the USA, you are not free do drive on the left side of the road, and you cannot choose not to pay for your train ride.

But according to Danish theologian and philosopher N. F. S. Grundtvig, we must have absolute freedom in all matters relating to the human conscience, and in everything that relates to our spiritual lives.[2] This explains why the prohibition against conversion in many Muslim countries is highly problematic. This prohibition within the sphere of human conscience is often maintained by Muslim families living in democratic countries, and it often results in adult children having to break all ties to their family due to personal conversion.

The specific question of *when* a child or young adult is free to leave the religious practice of the family will be treated later, in the section about children's intellectual freedom.

---

2. Grundtvig, *Nordens Mythologi*, 3–12.

To sum up, we have to make a clear distinction between *normal* social control, which is both necessary and productive, and *severe* social control, which adopts methods of stigmatization and isolation and interferes with individual freedom. We could define this distinction using the terms "*positive* social control" and "*negative* social control." However, I prefer two more distinct terms, as these are two highly distinct concepts. I suggest we speak of "social regulation" as something positive and "offensive control" as something negative. Changing a discourse is not easily done—but a clear distinction is of vital importance.

This distinction also makes us question to what extent we can equate the concepts of physical and psychological violence, and the concepts of force and control. The reasoning provided by critics of religious minorities is often that psychological violence can be placed alongside physical violence. But despite the similarities, it is important to make a clear distinction between issues that should involve the police and issues that should involve a therapist.

There is no doubt psychological violence is both offensive and damaging, but while physical violence is rather easy to identify, psychological violence is more complex. It is an act of physical violence to beat up your nine-year-old kid with a coat hanger, but it is not physical violence to grab your two-year-old firmly by the arm if he or she is about to step into traffic. Telling your teenage son he is a bad person because he supports a specific political party is clearly wrong, but is it psychological violence?

Although some degree of force is involved, it is not psychological violence to send your six-year-old to a Christian club, or to demand he or she comes with you to church on Sundays. The reason for this is that the opposite strategy—giving a minor the freedom to choose whether or not to take part in the religious practice of the family—would result in a more severe neglect, which would definitely lead to psychological damage. This would be an example of *desertion*.

This, however, does not mean we can, or should, control our children in every aspect of their spiritual lives. Even young children have the right to a private space where adults cannot enter without an invitation. But we are dealing with an extremely fine balance, and a close relationship with the child is necessary in order for us to properly judge when to intervene and when to set free.

THREATS OF HELL AND DAMNATION

Fundamentally, upbringing is a form of regulation. It always takes place in the context of a community and a culture—within the family, the local society, in communities of interest, or within a national culture—and it is a useful process, as we all depend on being part of a safe and healthy community.

At the same time, the *aim* of upbringing is to generate independence. This duality is called the "pedagogical paradox." The paradox is we have to find our point of departure in the dependence of the child, through upbringing, education, and influence, in order to strengthen the child's independence and emancipation. In other words, children need a firm foundation, something they can at least distance themselves from. However, if the child's upbringing is driven by absolute dependence, it results in a destructive form of control. As an example of social control or psychological violence, I have mentioned children and teenagers, in some church environments, are threatened with the prospect of hell when they do or say something wrong. In relation to children, this can be due to disobedience or lying, and in relation to young adults, such threats can be caused by disagreements regarding premarital sex or intentions of leaving the Christian community.

And yes, threatening with hell because your child says or does something wrong is a drastic thing to do. But if we dig a bit further, the issue becomes more nuanced. There is a significant difference between using hell as a threat and maintaining there is perdition for those who renounce their faith in God, even though none of us can determine what happens to the individual when we leave this world.

When critics claim all talk of perdition is a form of social control or psychological violence, their argumentation is based on a specific precondition, namely, in reality there is no such thing as life after death. Of course it is wrong to threaten people with things that are not real, but if you base your worldview on the words of Jesus and truly believe death leads us all in one of two directions, then it would be both dishonest and unloving to hide this conviction from the younger generation. Again, the crucial element is not the *content* of the claim but the *manner* in which it is communicated.

A fifteen-year-old should hear it formulated in a different way than a five-year-old, and it should never be the central theme in a Christian upbringing. Also, it might be a topic that belongs in Christian homes, rather than in Christian schools, but choosing *silence* would result in desertion and neglect. Without further comparison, you also let down your children by not warning them against smoking or playing around with explosives.

There are examples of parents, teachers, and preachers who have threatened with perdition, but such examples of abuse do not remove the possibility of a correct usage. Again, it is not the content of the conviction that in itself is offensive or an expression of social control but the manner, the method, or the timing *can* be. What will help a parent, teacher, or preacher to confront without intimizing and to withdraw without deserting is a careful consideration and inclusion of love and truth. This is also the case when it comes to communicating the reality of perdition to children and young adults.

At the same time, it is important that religious minorities inspire independent thought and honesty in the younger generation. It has to be legitimate to share your doubts regarding your faith. If we create dishonest environments where we cannot speak our mind, it strangles the intellectual and spiritual freedom of our homes, schools, and churches. This keeps our faith and convictions from growing stronger, as a forced faith is no faith at all.

In a healthy community, having a firm framework of guidelines to lean against is a positive thing, but if the framework is all there is, then it can happen that our inner lives will suffocate. We don't build our faith on the absence of doubt. Our faith is a firm trust although he often seems far away. We trust in a Creator whom we find it reasonable to believe in but whom we also still have a lot of questions for.

NEUTRALITY IS NOT AN OPTION

Evidently, there are both past and present examples of church communities where the upbringing of children has been characterized by both indoctrination and intimization, and where the intellectual freedom of children has been violated.[3] However, I do believe the criticism of these environments does not sufficiently consider one of the fundamental pedagogical realities, namely, children can only go through a healthy and independent development if the adult generation presents them with their own idea of the good life. We simply have to influence our children in order for them to become independent adults, but it has to be done with respect.

In addition, it is naive to believe the agnosticism and religious relativism of mainstream culture are neutral positions that automatically eliminate the risk of indoctrination, social control, and force. This is far from true. The only difference is the indoctrination of minority groups is easier to spot than that of the majority.

The nature of human life makes neutrality impossible. Everyone influences their children. They can't not do it. The central issue is whether or not it is done with respect. Learning to influence with respect is crucial to the minority as well as the majority.

We must fight for the intellectual freedom of our children, but in that struggle we must keep in mind our fundamental pedagogical principle, namely, the child can only take over the adult responsibility and independence through a slow and successive process.

RIGHTS AND OBLIGATIONS

On the one hand, we have the parents' right to influence their child politically and religiously in the child's best interest. On the other

---

3. Pedersen, *Påvirkning med respekt*, 65–153.

hand, we have the fundamental rights of the child. So, is the child autonomous when it comes to faith and personal convictions?

The answer is yes, but the autonomy is *relative to the child's age and maturity*. This perspective is clearly expressed in *The UN Convention on the Rights of the Child* from 1989:

> *Article 3, unit 1.* In all actions concerning children, whether undertaken by public or private social welfare institutions, courts of law, administrative authorities or legislative bodies, the best interests of the child shall be a primary consideration.
>
> *Article 12, unit 1.* States Parties shall assure to the child who is capable of forming his or her own views the right to express those views freely in all matters affecting the child, the views of the child being given due weight in accordance with the age and maturity of the child.
>
> *Article 14, unit 2.* States Parties shall respect the rights and duties of the parents and, when applicable, legal guardians, to provide direction to the child in the exercise of his or her right in a manner consistent with the evolving capacities of the child.

Reading article 14, it is striking that the child's process of learning to use its individual rights depends on parents or guardians guiding and instructing the child. No upbringing takes place in a value-neutral vacuum.

If we paint with a broad brush, recent years have brought about a shift of focus from *the rights of the parents and the duties of the child* to *the rights of the child and the duties of the parents*. In many ways, this shift has been both necessary and productive, as the rights of the child have been severely overlooked throughout history. But today, the danger consists in overlooking the rights of the parents. This distribution of rights is a fine balance, and putting too much weight on one side leads to trouble. At the very least it is extremely important, in a time where the primary focus is on the rights of the child, to maintain the rights of the parent, not only to protect the parent but also to protect *the child*.

The decisive factor we must consider is the young child is not yet of legal age or fully independent. The child's situation is determined by its immaturity. It can be discussed what age is the correct age of majority, but the very fact such a legal transition exists shows we are dealing with a gradual development toward a point where society deems the child mature enough for the parental rights to come to an end.

THE INTELLECTUAL FREEDOM OF THE CHILD

Today, most educational theories have abandoned the idea of a neutral upbringing. Instead, it seems more realistic and constructive to assume influence is a necessity in order for the child to obtain independence.

But in order for that to happen, the influencing must be rooted in freedom and respect for the child. Even young children need a certain amount of freedom. And it is important that this freedom is handed over to the child successively so the child gradually learns to handle and implement its individual rights, which the child holds at all stages of life. But this transfer of responsibility must take place in accordance with the age and maturity of the child.

The mutual relationship between the intellectual freedom of the parents and the child is illustrated in figure 8.

INFLUENCE WITH RESPECT

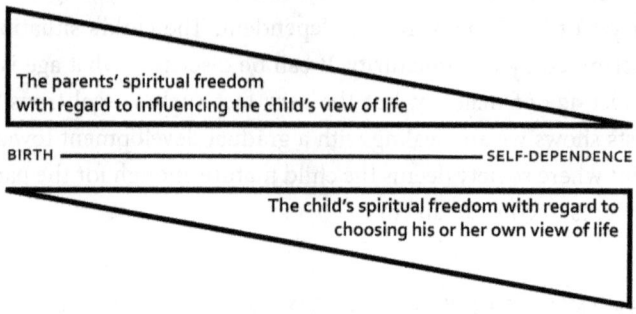

Fig. 8

We might say the child has a *dual right*: to be met with the best values known to the parents, and to freely take a stand on those values. In this way, the child gradually learns to take full responsibility as he or she approaches the age of majority. Naturally, this process always unfolds through intimate interaction with other people.

In this process, the public system is not responsible for controlling or limiting the intellectual freedom of the parents. Rather, the role of the public system is to protect the weak part, namely, the child, from illegal neglect. For instance, the public authorities must ensure an adoptive child is placed in a good home, but it is not their job to screen out adoptive parents who hold certain political, religious, or anti-religious viewpoints. Such practice would be a violation of the intellectual freedom of the parents.

SECTISM

When looking for a constructive way of influencing with respect, it might be useful to turn to a rather old phenomenon, namely, *the sect*. The concept of *sectism* can help us characterize religious extremism and root it out.

According to Norwegian writer and philanthropist Dag Hareide,[4] a sect is characterized by the following ten traits:

---

4. Andersen, *I god tro*, 5.

1. The sect is the truth.
2. Enlightenment within the sect is hierarchical and esoteric.[5]
3. The sect develops its own language, which becomes a closed system.
4. Members change their identity at admission.
5. The sect takes social control.
6. The leader of the sect holds the power.
7. The sect has a strong and simplistic understanding of its enemies.
8. The sect nurtures and upholds an inner enemy.
9. In the sect, the end justifies the means.
10. Leaving the sect is sanctioned.

Niels Gunnar Holmberth has conducted a sociopsychological investigation among people who have left a more or less narrow religious community. He draws the following conclusion: " . . . the problem centers on how the tradition is communicated, rather than on the tradition and its content in itself."[6] In other words, the problem of sectism is not primarily rooted in the ideology or faith of the sect, but in the way in which these beliefs are shared with the world—a conclusion which confirms the claims made earlier in this chapter.

Holmberth also distinguishes between "the confident" and the "the too-confident" communicator. He claims the former does not stand in the way of his or her own message, while the latter does. For instance, the too-confident communicators are convinced God is always on their side in relation to the child:

> This means that in every conflict and religious discussion they see their own interpretation as superior. And it means that they are always the most qualified when it comes to evaluating content and methods of

---

5. Meaning: private; secret; belonging to the select few.
6. Holmberth, *Innanför eller utanför*, 32.

communication. With such preconditions, it is likely that a communicator will adopt an unyielding and dismissive position, which automatically "invalidates" all other individuals.

In our material, it is made clear that the communicator's attitude toward the receiver is crucial to whether or not the receiver accepts a certain tradition.[7]

Holmberth has interviewed people who, as adults, have left church communities due to the use of force, disengagement, and isolation. He claims those who abandon pietist circles often do so due to high demands regarding lifestyle, while those who leave charismatic circles often do so because of spiritual pressure and expectations.

Arne Tord Sveinall, who has written about pastoral care in relation to sect survivors, sees a tendency among young people who have a distant relationship with natural authorities. According to Sveinall, these individuals are often drawn toward other types of authorities, such as gurus:

> Some people long for an authority because then most decisions are already made, and I do not have to make as many difficult decisions myself. . . . A sect often appears as the perfect solution for the weak self.[8]

Sveinall claims there are two main factors that tie individuals to sects. The first is the sect retains its members in a sense of guilt. As Freud says: "The human sense of guilt is the direct path to all manipulation."[9] The other factor is the sect, in a harmful manner, attaches its members to the strong, charismatic leader of the sect. This attachment often lures the individual member into a subtle process that in many ways is similar to depression.

Although the above-mentioned observations and analyses are rather old, they can still help us distinguish between healthy and unhealthy influence, and help us avoid the methods that

7. Holmberth, *Innanför eller utanför*, 165.
8. Sveinall, "Sjelesorg med sektoverlevende," 8.
9. Sveinall, "Sjelesorg med sektoverlevende," 8.

characterize religious extremism and radicalization. In addition, they can help us emphasize that minorities, within a democracy, hold a self-evident right to communicate their faith and convictions to their children, and to live out the personal consequences of these convictions, which is both natural and necessary for the sake of the children, teenagers, and grown-ups.

Chapter 6

WHAT OPTIONS DO PARENTS, TEACHERS, AND PREACHERS HAVE?

As we have already established, there are many factors at work when we influence others. Therefore, it is neither possible nor desirable to come up with a fixed manual for how to influence with respect. However, this complexity does not make it impossible to say something true about what parents, teachers, welfare workers, and preachers can do to ensure a positive form of influence.

Firstly, it is crucial those who carry a pedagogical responsibility become aware of both the positive and negative mechanisms at play within the sphere of influence. A primary aim of this book is to bring the reader closer to this awareness.

When this awareness has been established, the next aim is to lead the reader toward a growing empathy and maturity. These qualities are not uniquely pedagogical or Christian. Rather, they are universal character traits that are crucial to anyone who is directly engaged in upbringing, education, and preaching. I see these two personality traits as essential components in what we might call *the art of living*. All individuals are obliged to seek and practice these skills, including those of us who carry a pedagogical responsibility.

EMPATHY

Empathy is the ability to put yourself in someone else's place without giving up your own position. It is the ability to enter into the spirit of the other person and perceive questions and problems from their point of view. Empathy entails the ability to listen to others while being true to yourself.

But empathy is not simply an inborn human quality. It is a skill we can actively develop. The word *empathy* should not be confused with the word *sympathy*. Both words stem from the Greek word *pathos*, meaning *emotion*. The prefix "em-" means "in," while the prefix "sym-" means "with." Thus, empathy means "in-emotion," while sympathy means "with-emotion." This means you can have empathy for someone without having sympathy for them.

Fundamentally, empathy is the ability and will to perform a loop-movement, as illustrated in figure 9.

Fig. 9

As in the prior illustrations, A is the person with pedagogical responsibility, and B is the person who is being influenced.

The illustration depicts empathy as A's will and ability to leave his or her own familiar position and move into B's point of view in order to see the world from her perspective. What is B's emotional state after her parents' divorce? Why does B hold what to A appears to be an strange point of view? What images pop up in B's mind when I use words such as heaven or hell?

Most of us are only able to take another person's point of view for a moment, and this is how it should be. A must return to his or her own position, but with a new perspective, an increased understanding of B's personality. Through this process, A gets a better foundation for deciding what to say and what not to say.

In her book, *Empathy for Professionals*, Ulla Holm mentions a range of factors that influence our ability to express empathy. The first factor *is the development of our own identity and our relation to others*. This includes the development of *the object constancy*. This term refers to our ability to perceive another person as constant or stable, regardless of the context, emotions, and needs we experience in that moment. Holm says:

> Empathy depends . . . on the ability to decentralize, i.e. the ability to perceive oneself objectively. Decentralization, introspection, the development of observational skills, and a stable sense of identity are all preconditions for the necessary fluctuation between emotional experience and intellectual assessment that empathy entails.[1]

The second factor is *perspective-taking and interpretation of emotional expression*. "Perspective-taking is partly based on a person's ability to interpret the information conveyed through body language—facial expressions, posture, gestures and tone of voice."[2] This is an essential ability to possess if we want to avoid letdowns. As a preacher, perspective-taking is expressed through the ability to put yourself in the listener's situation and truly perceive an issue from his or her point of view. Here, the ability to decode someone's body language from the pulpit can be a vital skill.

The third factor Holm mentions is *affect-management*, which refers to our ability to handle our own emotions. In order to develop empathy, it is important that we are in contact with our own emotions. This is not the same as being controlled by our emotions. In fact, we can only learn to manage our own emotions if we understand them well and are familiar with them.

1. Holm, *Empati for professionelle*, 105–6.
2. Holm, *Empati for professionelle*, 108

The fourth factor is *affect tolerance*. This term refers to the ability to correctly identify other people's emotions. For instance, a teacher is easily tempted to misname a student's emotions in order to avoid a more serious challenge. It is often more convenient to identify a child's grief as mere weariness, or to identify a child who deals with anger as short-tempered. In short, our empathy also depends on *our courage* to correctly identify other people's emotions—and to act in accordance with them.

The fifth factor is *affect capacity*, i.e., having the capacity to embrace other people's emotions. This entails being able to enter into other people's emotions without being overwhelmed by them. This ability is important if we want to make B feel safe enough to express his or her emotions. "Empathy depends on our capacity to embrace the other person's emotions—a skill that, in turn, is nurtured through an empathic understanding of the emotional condition of the other person."[3]

Holm also mentions four impediments to empathy:

1. Emotional or social shortcomings in the early development of A's identity. The development of A's personality is premature.

2. Unconscious conflicts that activate rigid mental defense mechanisms. A deals with unresolved conflicts that disturb his empathic sensitivity.

3. Reduced awareness of emotional signals and reduced understanding of emotions as communicators of knowledge.

4. A's lack of motivation. For instance, A does not see it as his task to show empathy, or he claims he is too busy, or B does not deserve it.[4]

While the first three impediments relate to *the ability* to show empathy, the fourth relates to *the will* to show empathy. In order for parents, teachers, and preachers to develop empathy, they must be aware of these impediments and seek to overcome them. Generally, this aim is most easily reached through dialogue.

3. Holm, *Empati for professionelle*, 116.
4. Holm, *Empati for professionelle*, 128.

Today, however, there is a tendency toward an excessive psychologization, which is often used as a shield against other people. Empathy *is* an important skill, but it can be used in the wrong way. This happens when we use it to scrutinize other people's motives rather than to understand them, or when the honest care for the individual is undermined by an often intriguing psychological analysis of the other person's thoughts and actions.

Our empathy is fundamentally related to our curiosity and freedom from prejudice. Empathy is an honest interest in other people and a genuine desire to get to know and understand them better—an attitude that often enriches our own lives as well. To show empathy, we must let go of our prejudice and abstain from judging others before we get to know them, and before we understand their incentives.

However, freedom from prejudice is not the same as giving up your own opinions. In fact, it is possible for us to bring our political, religious, and moral standpoints into the encounter with others without judging them prematurely. In this light, empathy is something that springs from the fundamental idea that we are in a constant learning process, and we can always learn something new through the encounter with others.

MATURITY

Maturity is a personal quality we develop over time. However, this does not mean the oldest person is always the most mature. There are immature seventy-year-olds and mature thirty-year-olds. Maturity has to do with learning how to process your own experience and knowledge in order to obtain a more nuanced and humble view of life. However, maturity is also the process of finding an inner peace and a sense of certainty that, for instance, makes it easier for us to acknowledge our own strengths.

Relationship therapist Finn Korsaa writes about "the mature man," but these characteristics are equally applicable to mature women, and they are particularly important for men and women who carry a pedagogical responsibility. According to Korsaa, a mature person:

- calmly accepts that the often carefree and pleasure-driven lifestyle of childhood and adolescence has been replaced by the obligations and responsibilities of adulthood.
- can live together with people who hold opinions and viewpoints that deviate from his or her own.
- is more focused on his or her own situation than on everyone else's.
- takes responsibility for his or her relationships, even when it seems unfair, and is not afraid to hold other people responsible when necessary.
- always refrains from bad excuses—and mostly from good excuses as well.
- admits he or she is dependent on his or her closest friends and relatives.
- puts long-term goals and gains before short-term advantages.
- admits the evil and negative elements in his or her life cannot, at present, be ascribed to others but are mostly self-inflicted, and that this is a fact of life.
- is able to cope with other people's frustrations and anger, even when he or she is part of the problem.
- constantly practices his or her ability to accept the difficult and wonderful life he or she has been given.
- constantly seeks to renounce the envy he or she feels toward those who appear to have a better life.[5]

It is my conviction that people who possess several of these skills will usually be able to influence others in positive and legitimate ways.

In general, we must remind ourselves we should never develop our ability to influence in order to fulfill our personal desires,

---

5. Korsaa, *Naturens muntre søn*, 207–10.

such as our need for confirmation or power. A person who holds a pedagogical responsibility should, ideally, always be driven by something outside himself, something that in itself is significant and powerful enough to convince the receiver. When this is the case, the focus on A's ability to *persuade* is replaced by a focus on the *convincing* power of the message itself.

It is also crucial whether a person with pedagogical responsibility expands or diminishes the surrounding world for those he influences. To ensure you expand the perspective of those you influence, you must have a broad insight and interest in society in general and never avoid contact with people who hold different viewpoints.

But our ability to expand people's perspective also depends on whether or not we ourselves have a firm, personal standpoint—a platform from which we view the world. If this is not the case, it often leads to insecurity in our children, students, or listeners. It is therefore important that parents, teachers, and preachers seek to balance a broad orientation and insight with a careful contemplation of their own standpoint. Too much of the former tends to make us unreliable, and too much of the latter puts us in danger of sectarianism.

A significant factor in the psychology of intimization is the interplay between, for instance, a teacher and a group of students in which the majority share the teacher's viewpoint. The most significant influencing is often conducted by zealous students and not by the teacher. Of course, these students are often motivated by their own insecurity and need for confirmation.

In such situations, the teacher's maturity is crucial. He or she must hold the majority off and support those students who are under pressure. It is the teacher's responsibility to make room for the opinions of the minority. The teacher must challenge the majority and guide them toward a deeper consideration of their own standpoint.

Perhaps, the most important indicator of respectful influence is that the room in which it takes place is marked by a free and open atmosphere. It is a sign of maturity on behalf of the person holding the pedagogical responsibility when he or she is able to create an atmosphere that combines clarity with freedom.

HOW DO WE HELP EACH OTHER TO INFLUENCE WITH RESPECT?

However, the responsibility of influencing with respect does not only belong to the individual parent, teacher, or preacher. It is also an institutional responsibility, and it must partly be lifted by the schools, nursery schools, and churches in which the influencing takes place. It is a collective responsibility, and we must lift it together as we support and challenge each other to influence in a positive way.

Institutions and associations are therefore responsible for teaching their members and volunteers how to influence with respect. From here, the challenge is to create and uphold a collective climate and environment where people are willing to give and receive feedback on the influencing that takes place within the group. Let me give you a couple examples:

At home: If you and your spouse are close friends with other couples with children, it might be beneficial to have an open conversation about Christian influencing. Perhaps some of your friends need to be challenged and encouraged to practice a more Christian profile—this might be in relation to sharing their faith with their children or attending church. Others might need to consider if they are pushing their children too hard.

At school: If you are a teacher at a Christian school who is responsible for communicating the Christian message in class, but you never address the more serious implications of the Christian worldview, then it might be appropriate if your colleagues challenge you to do so.

In kindergarten: If a colleague corrects a child in a manner that you find inappropriate, then you might have to carefully tell your colleague how you experienced the situation. Or, if you believe your colleague should have confronted a child with its behavior, the best thing might be to talk about it.

At church: If you are one of two or three pastors in the same church, you can help each other to see whether you withdraw too much when it comes to speaking with authority, or whether you tend to be too pushy and presumptuous, making it hard for your listeners to feel free. In a similar manner, the congregation should be able to discuss such issues with their pastors and preachers.

In the children's club: In this context, we can also use the model for how to influence with respect as a foundation for an honest and considerate conversation about how we treat children.

In situations where we, as leaders of a school or a children's club, repeatedly experience a colleague intimizing or deserting, we ought to address it, either in that moment or in private. If the conversation has no effect, it might be necessary to initiate a more formal mentorship in order to help that colleague change a negative pattern.

That being said, we should always be careful not to constantly chase each other down. One of the pitfalls of presenting a model for how to influence with respect is we tend to become too aware of other people's flaws and shortcomings. "He is intimizing!" "She is deserting!" Of course, this is not the intention. The model is primarily meant for personal examination and inspiration, not as a tool for placing blame. However, such potential pitfalls do not exclude the possibility of putting it to use in a constructive manner on an institutional and collective level.

TWO KEY POINTS

I want to conclude this chapter by giving two key points that sum up the options available to A when it comes to influencing B in a positive manner:

- A must have a clear message. She must be passionate about something. She can be passionate about specific subject matter, a vision for a school, or leading children and young adults toward an acknowledgment of what is good, true, and beautiful in life. A can also be passionate about a political conviction, philosophical obligation, moral standpoint, or her faith in God. A must be motivated by something that is located outside and above herself. In other words, she must fundamentally be pointing away from herself, toward something more important.

- A must seek a positive dialogue with B. She must not be passionate about something in a manner that makes B seem unimportant. She must be characterized by a receptive openness, but also by a strong critical sense. She must strive to increase her own empathy and maturity. A must never use B as a means for her own ends—neither to cover up her own insecurity nor to confirm her own convictions. A must always want what is best for B, even when this is not something that *pleases* B.

Chapter 7

WHAT CAN CHILDREN, STUDENTS, AND LISTENERS DO?

LET US BEGIN BY taking another look at our basic model for how to influence with respect, i.e., influencing in the grey area in figure 6:

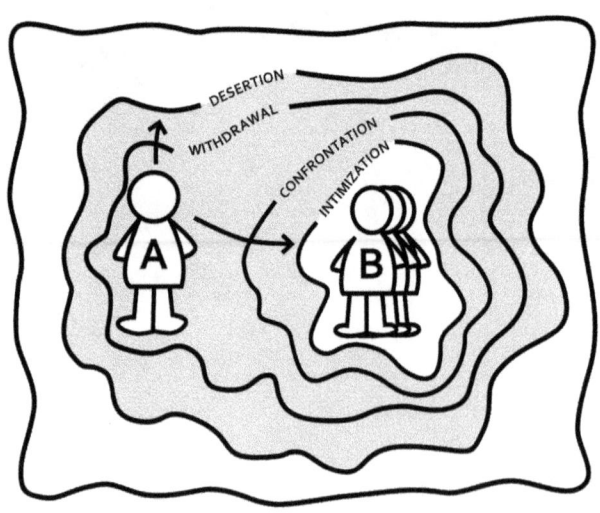

Fig. 6

Generally, A is responsible for making sure the influence is carried out with respect, but B also carries a responsibility. We

will now take a closer look at this mutual responsibility, especially within the parent-child relationship.

HOW DO WE BEST EQUIP CHILDREN, YOUNG ADULTS, AND GROWN-UPS?

B can either be a child, a young adult, or grown-up, and therefore B's responsibility must always be determined in relation to his or her age and maturity level. In relation to young adults and grown-ups, the responsibility for breaking away from the intimization or desertion usually belongs to the individual, and it can often be done by confronting the parent, teacher, or preacher with his or her transgressive behavior. However, younger children do not have this option because they are not mature enough to identify the letdown, or to break away from it.

Therefore, adults carry a distinct responsibility for avoiding intimization and desertion in relation to minors. Desertion must especially be avoided because it, as mentioned earlier, is more difficult for the child to identify and react to than intimization is.

This is also true in relation to adults who for various reasons are weaker or more immature than others. These might be people with disabilities, refugees, or other individuals who temporarily are in a vulnerable situation, perhaps due to a state of grief. When influencing such individuals, A's responsibility increases.

The younger, weaker, and more immature a person or group of people is, the more cautious we must be when navigating within the sphere of influence.

When it comes to minors, it is crucial their primary guardians, usually their parents, practice a respectful form of influence. I am not claiming parents must be perfect. We cannot go through parenthood without intimizing or deserting our children from time to time—but as long as we are aware of it, admit it, and, when necessary, apologize for it, we can keep the negative effect at a minimum. Children are sturdy, and they can do just fine with imperfect, but honest, parents. Therefore, the respectful influence we provide our children with at home is the most efficient shield we can give them against disrespectful influence in their future lives.

Also, I believe it is both possible and important that we dare to *speak* to children, young adults, and grown-ups about positive and negative forms of influence. It is to some extent possible to equip others to better navigate within this sphere. In addition, it is important to remind both young adults and grown-ups of the responsibility they carry when it comes to actively *selecting and rejecting* the various forms of influence they encounter.

Let me emphasize we are only talking about circumstances where no legal violation is committed. Crimes such as incest, violence, and acts of serious physical offense are not part of the framework presented here.

HOW DO WE HELP CHILDREN AND YOUNG ADULTS ENDURE CONFRONTATION?

When learning how to deal with confrontation, the decisive factor is the children are exposed to respectful influence at home, in school, and at church, with the home being the primary arena. Largely, this is a matter of practice. If we use our hands a lot, our skin gets thicker, and the same is true when it comes to confrontation.

When children, regardless of age and maturity, are met with healthy confrontation, they also usually develop an ability to cope with such confrontation. The child experiences that even though the immediate confrontation might be uncomfortable, it is helpful in the long term as it also provides a strong and intimate experience of the parents' love and care as the foundation of family life.

At first, it seems contradictory that we should take children's sensitivity seriously (as discussed earlier) and, at the same time, help them become more resilient. But in reality these needs are two sides of the same coin.

Before children can learn how to endure confrontation, they must obtain the ability to distinguish between confrontation and intimization—without having to know these two words. Fundamentally, this is a matter of learning how to distinguish between

WHAT CAN CHILDREN, STUDENTS, AND LISTENERS DO?

what is acceptable and what is unacceptable. The key factor is the child learns how to establish his or her own boundaries in relation to other people. The three most important factors in learning this are:

1. That the child's guardians, especially their parents, respect the child's boundaries.
2. That the child experiences its guardians', especially their parents', personal boundaries.
3. That the child, through its guardians, especially their parents, is connected to a greater whole, something located above and outside both parties.

By interacting with these three factors, the child is able to establish their own boundaries over time. These will often be similar to those of the stable and caring guardian, but they are never identical.

Respecting a child's boundaries is not just a matter of refraining from intimization. It is also a matter of refraining from desertion, as it is always crucial for the child not to feel abandoned.

The encounter with the parents' personal boundaries is crucial to the development of the child's own healthy boundaries. Therefore, parents should never be reluctant to reveal and demonstrate their own boundaries in relation to the child. These boundaries can be of a very concrete nature, such as table manners, chores, or language, but as parents we have to remember we can only set up rules for our children we are able to comply with ourselves.

In other situations, we might be dealing with more general or abstract boundaries, pertaining to moral behavior, family traditions, or rules related to political or religious convictions. In this sphere, parents must be even more aware of the uselessness of trying to implement norms they themselves do not follow, or that they, if they fail, are not willing to *admit* to overstepping.

Because human existence is comprised of more than just our immediate, interpersonal relationships, it is also important the child is confronted with life in a larger context. Some will refer to this as the existential dimension of life, others as the moral, altruistic, or evolutionary dimension, and others again as the social or religious dimension. Here, I am primarily concerned with the Christian dimension.

Most people will experience a personal Christian faith as both a gift and an obligation. On the one hand, it gives us a perspective on our everyday lives. Our faith gives us something to live for apart from physical survival. On the other hand, our faith often feels like a task, an obligation that demands something of me, a calling I must adhere to.

In this context, it is also true the adult is unable to connect the child to something greater if he is not personally engaged in that conviction or belief. In addition, passing on the Christian faith to your children is primarily a matter of the way you live your life, rather than the words you speak—although they are important too.

When the children become teenagers and come of age, we can begin to talk to them about confrontation, withdrawal, intimization, and desertion. For instance, a way of helping a fifteen-year-old to better cope with confrontation might be to give him a brief psychological explanation of how the rules he must adhere to now, although they seem unfair and meaningless, will help develop his independence in the future.

Demonstrating *one's personal boundaries* while *respecting the child's own boundaries*—all within a framework of *general norms, life goals, limits, and faith*—is the best way for parents to teach their children how to distinguish between letdown and respect in relation to other adults, and how to endure the experience of legitimate confrontation.

HOW DO WE HELP CHILDREN AND YOUNG ADULTS DEAL WITH WITHDRAWAL?

Teaching our children how to deal with legitimate confrontation is not our only challenge. We must also do our best to show them how to cope with legitimate withdrawal. As with confrontation, legitimate withdrawal can lead to conflicting emotions and a sense of unease in the child. Here, the danger is not that the guardian comes too close, but that he or she becomes too distant.

In these cases, it is equally important to take the child's age into consideration. Obviously, the youngest children, who are fundamentally helpless, have a very limited capacity for withdrawal. This capacity slowly grows, and as the child gradually gains independence, he or she must also learn to deal with withdrawal in a constructive way.

Over time, the child's responsibility for his or her own behavior expands. The exterior "you must" must give way to the interior "I should." Mom and dad must slowly refrain from answering all questions regarding what one should and should not do. It often seems scary for a half-grown child to make such assessments alone, but mom and dad can help by explaining it is an exercise in independence and a step toward becoming your own person.

In the sphere of Christian influence, there are also children, teenagers, and young adults who need support and encouragement in learning to stand up for their own faith. Instead of providing perfect answers to all dogmatic and ethical questions, it might sometimes be better for a parent to point the child toward an article that discusses the issue, and then "we can discuss it later when you've thought about it yourself!"

When the withdrawal takes place in an atmosphere of trust and caring consideration, most children will also experience it as consistent with their own growing need for independence.

THREE CRUCIAL QUESTIONS TO CONSIDER AS A PARENT

This section presents three questions that are mainly directed at parents. The questions are tools for individual examination of the foundation we provide for the development of our child's own boundaries. Again, remember there are no universal answers when it comes to child rearing. Rather, what truly helps the child is that the parents find an individual approach they feel good about:

1. *Are we good at embracing our child's emotions?* In order for our child's development to be healthy, in relation to dealing with influence, it is important we acknowledge the child's emotions. This does not mean we should accept all forms of emotional expression, but all children need to be able to bring their emotions to their parents. This could be the child's grief over the death of the family dog, the anger over not being allowed to watch a football match, the joy of having made a new friend, or the surprise of seeing a flower suddenly in bloom.

    It is important that parents and other close adults notice and acknowledge these emotions, and that they *do not* silence them. However, the need to recognize the child's emotions does not diminish the adult's authority. As parents, we can show our child we recognize their anger while still maintaining—through confrontation—the child must hand back the toy to their playmate.

2. *Do we give our children a healthy self-confidence?* This question is also important in relation to the influences our children experience. A healthy self-esteem is more important than a healthy self-confidence. The self-esteem is nurtured when the child is seen and appreciated for what they *are*, not for what they *do*. But that does not mean a strong self-confidence is irrelevant. Self-confidence is the joy and satisfaction of being good at something, whether it is drawing, running, playing drums, building tree houses, or doing math. As parents, we should ask ourselves whether we show enough interest in our children's interests and abilities. Do we remember to praise and encourage them? And do we challenge them so their abilities can grow?

3. *Do we help our children become aware of the many implicit influences that surround them?* The child's ability to draw boundaries does not only depend on explicit influence from authorities such as teachers or parents. The implicit influence of the media and the child's peers is equally important. In

fact, I believe becoming aware of the implicit forms of influence also helps the child become more aware of the explicit forms.

Here, both children and adults need an ethical map to follow. How much energy should I spend becoming successful in the eyes of others? To what extent is life about pleasure? How important is it how I look? What nonmaterial values should define my life? We can find most of the answers to these questions in our faith or belief.

HOW DO WE HELP CHILDREN AND YOUNG ADULTS BREAK AWAY FROM INTIMIZATION?

Having to break away from intimization is very different from dealing with a legitimate confrontation, and therefore the supporting role of the parents or guardians also changes significantly.

Several of the informants previously mentioned in this book have stated it made a significant difference whether or not their parents supported them when they experienced intimization. Those who found support in their parents found it less difficult to break away from the intimization, whereas those who were not supported found it more difficult.

The interviews also revealed the form of parental support differed significantly in each case. Some were able to talk to their parents about their experiences at school. In other cases, the parents would go directly to the teacher to deal with the issue, and others again would tackle the issue by moving their child to a new school. However, one of my informants who found no support at home was still able to break away from the intimization he experienced, but he had to leave both his school and his congregation behind.

It goes without saying that the challenge of escaping intimization is most difficult and painful when those who cause it are not people outside the home, but the parents themselves, who are supposed to be the child's primary protectors from this form of influence. Nonetheless, experience has shown that, with support from others, most people will be able to overcome intimization. This is often a long process, and some are unable to gather the strength and courage to do it before they become adults.

In order to overcome intimization, it is crucial we break the vicious circle of shame and suppression. As several informants mention, one of the most difficult and painful consequences of intimization is the child accepts the self-image the adult presents them with: "I am stupid! I am not right! I am always guilty!"

Often, the idea that perhaps the adult is the guilty one is not even an option. The thought alone becomes a taboo that cannot be broken. Here, it is important that a caring adult steps in and helps the child break the taboo by talking openly about the intimization. The adult must help the child, teenager, or young adult realize he does not betray his parents by talking about these matters. In fact, talking about it is the only way to break free from it.

Protecting yourself from intimization can be an extensive and painful process. In some cases, it is necessary to seek help from a professional therapist—but these instances fall outside the framework of this book.

HOW DO WE HELP ADULTS BREAK AWAY FROM INTIMIZATION AND DEAL WITH CONFRONTATION?

Let us approach this question by looking at the sphere of preaching. It is not possible to set up general principles that can determine whether a sermon or lecture is confrontational (in a positive sense) or intimizing (in a negative sense). In fact, this issue is so complex that what might seem intimizing to some people is often perceived as a positive confrontation by others. But if we, as adults, repeatedly listen to a preacher who we experience as intimizing, it is our own responsibility to take action. The responsible reaction might simply be to stop listening to the specific preacher, perhaps temporarily, and instead find another congregation to join. But the appropriate response might also be to speak to the preacher or pastor in question and confront him or her with the elements you experience as transgressive.

WHAT CAN CHILDREN, STUDENTS, AND LISTENERS DO?

Perhaps, the listener needs to give the preacher or pastor a second chance, or perhaps the conversation reveals that the best solution, although this might be a painful realization, is to find another congregation to attend, at least for a while. In this situation, the adult listener must take full responsibility for his own decision.

This being said, I also believe there is a need today, where desertion has become a greater threat than intimization, to encourage both young people and adults to not be too sensitive, but instead to master their own vulnerability and learn how and when to mitigate it.

Naturally, such capacities are primarily determined by our emotions and cannot be fully controlled by reason. Nonetheless, it is possible to push our own limits and the limits of others a bit, especially by *talking* about them openly. Sometimes, a rational acknowledgment of the need to receive a serious and personal communication of the Christian message can help us cope with the confrontation and realize it is beneficial to us in the long run.

If what the preacher communicates is in fact true—meaning in accordance with God's revelation through his Son, Jesus Christ, and his word, the Bible, then this is more important than the emotional responses of those listening. This is a perspective both the preacher and listener must contemplate. If you are convinced an absolute truth exists, then you must also be ready to accept that the influence of that truth may come with a price. We must accept that a confrontation with this truth can be experienced as a form of pressure. But to ensure this pressure does not run wild, the communication of absolute truths must be accompanied by a strong sense of respect for the individual.

Five hundred years ago, Martin Luther came to the same realization. In a sermon, he said the following: "Summa summarum: Preach it I will. Say it I will. Write it I will. But I will never force it on anyone. For we put on our faith freely and without force."[1] In short, preachers must also be encouraged to perform healthy and timely withdrawals. They should never take the responsibility away from their listeners. Instead, they must let go and allow their

---

1. Luther, *Otte prædikener holdt i Wittenberg i fasten 1522*, 17.

listeners to find their own way and take responsibility before God. However, this awareness does not prevent confrontation. In fact, confrontation is always a precondition.

CHAPTER 8

LOVE REQUIRES NEARNESS AND DISTANCE

In modern psychology and educational theory, Kierkegaard is often quoted as saying that "If one is truly to succeed in leading a person to a specific place, one must first and foremost take care to find him where he is and begin there."[1] This statement is the title of §2 in the second part of Kierkegaard's autobiographical account, *The Point of View for My Work as an Author*. In this paragraph, he says the following:

> In order truly to help someone else, I must understand more than he—but certainly first and foremost understand what he understands. If I do not do that, then my greater understanding does not help him at all. If I nevertheless want to assert my greater understanding, then it is because I am vain or proud, then basically instead of benefiting him I really want to be admired by him.[2]

Here, Kierkegaard points to a central threat to all parents, teachers, club leaders, and preachers who influence others—namely, the danger of intimizing the other person by raising oneself above him or her. To avoid this, Kierkegaard urges us to be cautious when speaking to others.

1. Kierkegaard, *Point of View*, 45.
2. Kierkegaard, *Point of View*, 45.

But a bit further down, Kierkegaard makes another equally central point we often tend to overlook. If we move to §4, we come across the following title: "Even though a person refuses to go along to the place to which one is endeavoring to lead him, there is still one thing that can be done for him: compel him to become aware."[3] Thus, Kierkegaard does not only compel us to be cautious, but to show courage when we influence others through our words and actions. In the beginning of §4, Kirkegaard elaborates:

> Compel a person to an opinion, a conviction, a belief—in all eternity, that I cannot do. But one thing I can do . . . I can compel him to become aware. That this is a good deed, there is no doubt, but neither must it be forgotten that this is a daring venture. By compelling him to become aware, I succeed in compelling him to judge. Now he judges. But what he judges is not in my power. Perhaps he judges the very opposite of what I desire.[4]

This paragraph is as important as the former because it compels us to challenge others to take a stand, especially in relation to life's existential questions. If we stick to the terminology of this book, Kierkegaard stresses the importance of *confrontation*.

Just like the need to withdraw in order to avoid intimization, we also need to avoid desertion by daring to confront. Both capacities are necessary if we want to help children, young adults, grown-ups, students, and listeners find their own standpoint.

A LOVE THAT COMBINES NEARNESS AND DISTANCE

God has provided human life with a fundamental tension between nearness and distance. This tension reflects life's most fundamental relationship—the relationship between God and man.

---

3. Kierkegaard, *Point of View*, 49.
4. Kierkegaard, *Point of View*, 49.

The simple sentence, "So God created man in his own image..."[5] expresses this tension clearly. The distance is expressed in the fact that God created a *man*, not a god. God created a being who, like himself, is a person, but who by no means is a god. Nonetheless, he created this new being *in his own image*, and therefore man is uniquely similar to God.

This tension between distance and nearness continues throughout the biblical depiction of the relationship between God and man. On the one hand, God is deeply engaged in our individual lives and wishes to have fellowship with us; on the other hand, God grants us full autonomy and refrains from forcing us into fellowship with him. God confronts us with his justice as well as his love, but withdraws from us and tells us we are responsible for our relationship with him and with other people. However, to use my own terminology, God never deserts nor intimizes us.

It is this fundamental premise for the relationship between God and man that we, in a Christian context, must apply to our interpersonal relationships. In the following passage from the Gospel of Matthew, Jesus confirms this approach:

> You shall love the Lord your God with all your heart and with all your soul and with all your mind. This is the great and first commandment. And a second is like it: You shall love your neighbor as yourself.[6]

According to Jesus, the careful balance between distance and nearness is part of what defines love. We cannot love someone without allowing that other person to *be* himself. If we seek to swallow up the other person and erase his or her individuality, then the love becomes both meaningless and merciless. But at the same time, if we do not keep the other person near, the love becomes equally impossible. By definition, a neighbor is a fellow human being who is in close proximity to us. True love entails a need to be close to the other person, while still respecting the fact that the other person is entirely *another* person.

---

5. Gen 1:27 (ESV).
6. Matt 22:37–39 (ESV).

On this basis, we can see the boundaries that this book discusses as a result of man's divine origin as well as our present relationship with God and our fellow human beings.

In addition, it is a fundamental biblical idea that man's godlikeness is tied to God's own incarnation in Jesus Christ. The apostle Paul describes Jesus as ". . .the image of the visible God, the firstborn of all creation" and says "in him the whole fullness of deity dwells bodily."[7] Thus, Jesus is the ultimate expression of God's nearness and distance. The Eternal, Almighty, and Invisible God comes near to us by becoming a time-limited, vulnerable, and visible human being. But despite his incarnation he remains distant by never ceasing to be fully God.

The distance between us and Jesus also becomes evident when he says his kingdom is not of this world, and when he holds people responsible for their words and actions. While being limited by human history, geography, and biology, Jesus demonstrated a perfect love—a love that comes close, but is also combined with a distance caused by his respect for our individual responsibility. Jesus' respect for us is so strong it includes the freedom to reject him.

Those who follow him are called to practice a similar approach toward other people. Although we can never live up to the life of Jesus, the New Testament encourages us to follow in his footsteps—also within the sphere of influence.

Although the result will always be marked by our imperfection, we must pick up the challenge of balancing nearness and distance in our interaction with others. This is a matter of daring to engage in healthy confrontation for the sake of our fellow human being, while at the same time seeking never to subvert the other person's self-agency. And it is a matter of withdrawing—again, for the sake of our fellow human being—but without leaving anyone to themselves. With help from these simple tools, it is my sincere hope you will find the wisdom and courage to master this fine balance.

---

7. Col 1:15, and 2:9 (ESV).

BIBLIOGRAPHY

Adfærdskontrol og tankefængsel. Copenhagen: Børns Vilkår, 2019.
Andersen, Rune. *I god tro—erfaringskonferanse om barns oppvekst i isolerte trossamfunn.* Oslo: Redd Barna, 2002.
Grundtvig, N. F. S. *Nordens Mythologi.* Copenhagen: J. H. Schubothes, 1832.
Hansen, Nils Gunder. *Lille dreng med rejseskrivemaskine.* Copenhagen: Kristeligt Dagblads Forlag, 2011.
Holm, Ulla. *Empati for professionelle.* Copenhagen: Hans Reitzels Forlag, 2003.
Holmberth, Nils Gunnar. *Innanför eller utanför. En socialpsykologisk undersöking av ifrågasättandet av religiös tradition och grupptillhörighet.* Uppsala: Acta Universitatis Upsaliensis Psychologia Religionum 9, 1980.
Horten, Torbjørn. "Udsigt over Ungdomsskolens udvikling." In *Menneskesyn, danning, kristen forkynning i Folkehøgskolen,* edited by Asbjørn Tveiten, and Bjarne Kvam, 84–85. Bergen, Norway: Norsk Lærerakademi, 1983.
Hvas, Søren Lodberg. *Folkeskolens kristendomsundervisning—Begrundelse og opgave.* Copenhagen: Gyldendal, 1974.
Kierkegaard, Søren. *The Point of View for My Work as an Author.* Edited and translated by Howard H. Hong and Edna H. Hong. Princeton: Princeton University Press, 1998.
Korsaa, Finn. *Naturens muntre søn: Portræt af den moderne mand.* Copenhagen: Lindhardt & Ringhof, 2017.
Luther, Martin. "Otte prædikener holdt i Wittenberg i fasten 1522." In *Luthers skrifter i udvalg, bind II,* edited by Regin Prenter, 10–45. Aarhus, Denmark: Aros, 1980.
Mollenhauer, Klaus. *Glemte sammenhenger. Om kultur og oppdragelse.* Oslo: Ad notam Gyldendal, 1996.
Myhre, Reidar. *Hva er pedagogikk?* Oslo: Gyldendal Norsk Forlag, 1982.
———. *Innføring i pedagogikk 2. Skole- og undervisningsteori.* Oslo: Fabritius Forlagshus, 1978.
Pedersen, Carsten Hjorth. *Påvirkning med respekt. Skoleliv mellem intimisering og desertering.* Copenhagen: Gyldendal, 2007.

BIBLIOGRAPHY

Sandsmark, Signe. *Is World View Neutral Education Possible and Desirable?: A Christian Response to Liberal Arguments.* Nottingham, UK: Paternoster, 2000.

Sveinall, Arne Tord. "Sjelesorg med sektoverlevende." *IKON* 19 (juni 1997) 7–10.

Tønnesen, Finn Egil. *Verdier og livssyn i skole og barnehage.* Oslo: J.W. Cappelens Forlag, 1983.

ABOUT THE AUTHOR

Married to Ellen since 1982.

Father of three children, born in 1984, 1986, and 1991.

Youth ministry leader since 1970.

Preacher to adult audiences since 1975.

Certified teacher since 1980.

Teacher/headmaster at a Christian free school from 1983–89 and 1996–99.

Daily leader of the Danish Christian Institute of Education since 1999.

Lector in educational theory since 2004.

Author of more than twenty books on upbringing, education, and preaching.

www.ingramcontent.com/pod-product-compliance
Lightning Source LLC
Chambersburg PA
CBHW070509090426
42735CB00012B/2707